ARM 55 Course Guide

Risk Control
2nd Edition

American Institute for Chartered Property Casualty Underwriters/Insurance Institute of America

720 Providence Road · Suite 100 · Malvern, PA 19355-3433

Second Edition · First Printing · August 2008

ISBN 978-0-89463-371-3

Contents

Study Materials Available for ARM 55

Richard Berthelsen and James Kallman, *Risk Control,* 1st ed., 2005, AICPCU/IIA.

ARM 55 *Course Guide,* 2nd ed., 2008, AICPCU/IIA (includes access code for SMART Online Practice Exams).

ARM 55 SMART Study Aids—Review Notes and Flash Cards, 2nd ed.

Student Resources

Catalog A complete listing of our offerings can be found in *Succeed*, the Institutes' professional development catalog, including information about:

- Current programs and courses
- Current textbooks, course guides, and SMART Study Aids
- Program completion requirements
- Exam registration

To obtain a copy of the catalog, visit our Web site at www.aicpcu.org or contact Customer Service at (800) 644-2101.

How To Pass Institute Exams! This free handbook, printable from the Student Services Center on the Institutes' Web site at www.aicpcu.org, or available by calling Customer Service at (800) 644-2101, is designed to help you by:

- Giving you ideas on how to use textbooks and course guides as effective learning tools
- Providing steps for answering exam questions effectively
- Recommending exam-day strategies

Institutes Online Forums Do you wish you could talk with people around the country about course questions and share information with others who have similar professional interests? We host forums at our Web site, where you can do just that. To access our forums:

- Go to the Institutes' Web site at www.aicpcu.org
- Click on the "Log on. Learn." link
- Scroll down and click on "Forums"
- Read the instructions, and you're ready to go!

Educational Services To ensure that you take courses matching both your needs and your skills, you can obtain advice from the Institutes by:

- E-mailing your questions to advising@cpcuiia.org
- Calling an Institutes' advisor directly at (610) 644-2100, ext. 7601

- Obtaining, completing, and submitting a self-inventory form, available on our Web site at www.aicpcu.org or by contacting Customer Service at (800) 644-2101

Exam Registration Information As you proceed with your studies, be sure to arrange for your exam.

- Consult the registration booklet that accompanied this course guide for complete information regarding exam dates and fees worldwide. Plan to register with the Institutes well in advance of your exam to take advantage of any discounted rates.
- If your registration booklet does not include exam dates for the current year, you can obtain up-to-date exam information by visiting the Institutes' Web site at www.aicpcu.org, sending an e-mail to customerservice@cpcuiia.org, or calling the Institutes at (800) 644-2101.

How to Contact the Institutes For more information on any of these publications and services:

- Visit our Web site at www.aicpcu.org
- Telephone us at (800) 644-2101 or (610) 644-2100 outside the U.S.
- E-mail us at customerservice@cpcuiia.org
- Fax us at (610) 640-9576
- Write us at AICPCU/IIA, Customer Service, 720 Providence Road, Suite 100, Malvern, PA 19355-3433

Using This Course Guide

This course guide will help you learn the course content and pass the exam.

Each assignment in this course guide typically includes the following components:

Educational Objectives These are the most important study tools in the course guide. Because all of the questions on the exam are based on the Educational Objectives, the best way to study for the exam is to focus on these objectives.

Each Educational Objective typically begins with one of the following action words, which indicate the level of understanding required for the exam:

Analyze—Determine the nature and the relationship of the parts.

Apply—Put to use for a practical purpose.

Calculate—Determine numeric values by mathematical process.

Classify—Arrange or organize according to class or category.

Compare—Show similarities and differences.

Contrast—Show only differences.

Define—Give a clear, concise meaning.

Describe—Represent or give an account.

Evaluate—Determine the value or merit.

Explain—Relate the importance or application.

Identify or list—Name or make a list.

Illustrate—Give an example.

Justify—Show to be right or reasonable.

Paraphrase—Restate in your own words.

Summarize—Concisely state the main points.

Required Reading The items listed in this section indicate what portion of the study materials (the textbook chapter(s), course guide readings, or other assigned materials) correspond to the assignment.

Outline The outline lists the topics in the assignment. Read the outline before the required reading to become familiar with the assignment content and the relationships of topics.

Key Words and Phrases These words and phrases are fundamental to understanding the assignment and have a common meaning for those working in insurance. After completing the required reading, test your understanding of the assignment's key words and phrases by writing their definitions.

For help, refer to the page numbers that appear in parentheses after each key word and phrase.

Review Questions The review questions test your understanding of what you have read. Review the Educational Objectives and required reading, then answer the questions to the best of your ability. When you are finished, check the answers at the end of the assignment to evaluate your comprehension.

Application Questions These questions continue to test your knowledge of the required reading by applying what you've studied to real-life situations. Again, check the suggested answers at the end of the assignment to review your progress.

Sample Exam The sample exam helps you test your knowledge of the material. Use the sample exam at the back of the course guide or the SMART Online Practice Exams to become familiar with the test format. A printable sample national exam is included as part of the SMART Online Practice Exams product. Once you have activated the course using the access code found on the inside back cover of this course guide, you can download and print a sample national exam. The Online Practice Exams product also allows you to take full practice exams using the same software that you will use when you take your national exam.

More Study Aids

The Institutes also produce supplemental study tools, called SMART Study Aids, for many of their courses. When SMART Study Aids are available for a course, they are listed on both page iii of this course guide and on the first page of each assignment. SMART Study Aids include review notes and flash cards and are excellent tools to help you learn and retain the information contained in each assignment.

ARM Advisory Committee

The following individuals were instrumental in helping to analyze the audience for the ARM program and to design the revisions and updates of the study materials for ARM 55.

Patricia M. Arnold, CPCU, ALCM
University of Texas at Austin

Bryan W. Barger, CPCU, ARM, ALCM
Marsh USA, Inc.

Karen L. Butcher, ARM
Aon Risk Services, Inc. of Ohio

Dr. Richard B. Corbett, CLU, CPCU, ARM
Florida State University

Donald E. Dresback, CPCU, ARM, AAI
The Beacon Group, Inc.

Mary M. Eisenhart, CPCU, ARM, ARe
Agency Management—Resource Group

Elise M. Farnham, CPCU, ARM, AIM
Illumine Consulting

Edward S. Katersky, CPCU, ARM, CSP
BJ's Wholesale Club, Inc.

Melissa Olsen Leuck, ARM
TAP Pharmaceutical Products Inc.

Bill Mason, CPCU, ARM-P
Public Risk Management Association

Ludmilla Pieczatkowska, CPCU
William Gallagher Associates Insurance Brokers, Inc.

James Swanson, FIIC, RIMS Fellow
Government of Manitoba, Canada

Tom Worischeck, CSP, ARM
Kimmins Contrating Corp.

Direct Your Learning

Understanding Risk Control

Educational Objectives

After learning the content of this assignment, you should be able to:

1. Describe risk control and its importance to an organization and to the economy

2. Describe and illustrate the following theories and approaches of accident causation:

   a. Domino theory

   b. General methods of control approach

   c. Energy transfer theory

   d. Technique of operations review (TOR) approach

   e. System safety approach

3. Explain how to implement the following risk control techniques:

   a. Avoidance

   b. Loss prevention

   c. Loss reduction

   d. Separation, duplication, and diversification

4. Define or describe each of the Key Words and Phrases for this assignment.

Study Materials

Required Reading:
▶ Risk Control
  • Chapter 1

Study Aids:
▶ SMART Online Practice Exams
▶ SMART Study Aids
  • Review Notes and Flash Cards—Assignment 1

Outline

▶ **Risk Control and Its Importance**

▶ **Accident Causation**

    A. Domino Theory

    B. General Methods of Control Approach

    C. Energy Transfer Theory

    D. Technique of Operations Review (TOR) Approach

    E. System Safety Approach

▶ **Risk Control Techniques**

    A. Avoidance

    B. Loss Prevention

    C. Loss Reduction

    D. Separation, Duplication, and Diversification

▶ **Summary**

If you are not sure that you have the current edition of the textbook(s), course guide, or registration booklet for the exam you plan to take, please contact the Institutes (see page iv).

For each assignment, you should define or describe each of the Key Words and Phrases and answer each of the Review and Application Questions.

Educational Objective 1

Describe risk control and its importance to an organization and to the economy.

Key Word or Phrase

Risk control (p. 1.4)

Review Questions

1-1.   Identify three aspects of risk control techniques that are important in understanding how risk control preserves an organization's resources. (p. 1.4)

1-2.   Contrast how an organization's resources are preserved through risk control and risk financing. (p. 1.4)

1-3.   Explain the importance of matching a risk control technique with one or more specific loss exposures. (p. 1.5)

Application Question

1-4. After repeated break-ins, a boat dealer wants to protect his
       inventory from further theft and vandalism by placing a vicious
       guard dog on his lot during the hours his dealership is closed.
       The dog would be behind an eight-foot cyclone fence topped
       with barbed wire on a well-lit lot.

   a. What is the potential effect on the dealer's liability loss
      exposure to lawsuits if the guard dog injures someone?

   b. How does placing a guard dog on the premises affect the
      total cost of risk of the boat dealer?

   c. What other risk control measures might the boat dealer use
      to reduce his property loss exposures from theft and van-
      dalism that would probably not substantially increase his
      liability loss exposure?

Educational Objective 2

Describe and illustrate the following theories and approaches of accident causation:

a. Domino theory

b. General methods of control approach

c. Energy transfer theory

d. Technique of operations review (TOR) approach

e. System safety approach

Key Words and Phrases

Domino theory (p. 1.6)

General methods of control (p. 1.7)

Energy transfer theory (p. 1.8)

Technique of operations review (TOR) (p. 1.9)

System safety (p. 1.10)

Review Questions

2-1. Identify the chain of accident factors set out in the domino theory. (p. 1.6)

2-2.   Explain why H.W. Heinrich believed that removing the third domino in the domino theory of accident causation typically is the best way to prevent injury or illness. (p. 1.6)

2-3.   Explain how control methods can be applied in the general methods of control approach. (p. 1.8)

2-4.   State five principles of risk control that follow from the technique of operations review. (p. 1.10)

▶▶

Application Question

2-5.   Sam, a twenty-five-year-old house painter employed by Acme Construction Company, almost fell from a ladder two weeks ago while painting the gutters of a nearly completed new house. Working fast to finish before quitting time, Sam was reaching far to his left to finish the last section rather than taking the time to climb down the ladder and move it. Because Sam had inadequately braced the ladder, and because the apprentice who worked with Sam was out sick and everyone else was too busy to watch the ladder, no one noticed the base of the ladder slipping out to Sam's right. As the ladder fell, Sam caught himself on the gutter with his right hand but—after hanging there for a few seconds—dropped to the ground as the gutter gave way under his weight. Although the collapsing gutter slowed his fall, Sam landed crookedly—his right hand extended above his head, his left leg hitting the ground first. Describe how each of the following theories would apply to this loss:

a. The domino theory

b. The general methods of control approach

c. The energy transfer theory

d. The technique of operations review (TOR) approach

e. The system safety approach

Educational Objective 3

Explain how to implement the following risk control techniques:

a.   Avoidance

b.   Loss prevention

c.   Loss reduction

d.   Separation, duplication, and diversification

Key Words and Phrases

Avoidance (p. 1.11)

Loss prevention (p. 1.12)

Loss reduction (p. 1.13)

Separation (p. 1.13)

Duplication (p. 1.14)

Diversification (p. 1.14)

Review Questions

3-1.   Under what circumstances would avoidance be an appropriate
       risk control technique? (p. 1.12)

3-2.   Describe how the risk control technique of loss prevention dif-
       fers from the following risk control techniques:

       a. Avoidance (p. 1.12)

       b. Loss reduction (p. 1.13)

3-3.   Describe the two categories of loss reduction measures. (p. 1.13)

3-4.   Explain how separation of an asset or operation differs from
       duplication of an asset or operation. (pp. 1.13–1.14)

Application Question

3-5.   The managers of a school district in rural New England are concerned that the district may not have enough fuel oil to heat its schools during the severe winter months and, therefore, it may lose its state and federal subsidies for failing to provide the mandated 180 days of education. Such a fuel shortage may arise in some future years because of either the excessive cost or the total unavailability of fuel oil for schools.

The risk management professional for the school district has been asked to offer his recommendations for a five-year plan for the district to overcome this exposure to loss of state and federal funds. The risk management professional believes that this loss exposure is one to which at least some risk management techniques can be properly applied. For each of the following risk management techniques, explain why that technique could or could not be used by the school district to overcome this loss exposure:

a. Avoidance

b. Loss prevention

c. Loss reduction

d. Separation and duplication of exposure units

Answers to Assignment 1 Questions

NOTE: These answers are provided to give students a basic understanding of acceptable types of responses. They often are not the only valid answers and are not intended to provide an exhaustive response to the questions.

Educational Objective 1

1-1.   Three aspects of risk control techniques that are important in understanding how risk control preserves an organization's resources are as follows:

(1) They focus on actual harm.

(2) They are measured only from a given entity's perspective.

(3) They need to be matched to specific loss exposures.

1-2.   An organization's resources are preserved in the following ways:

- Risk control—focuses on actual harm and is concerned with the fact that the harm occurred, not with the fact that it has been financially mitigated.

- Risk financing—focuses on obtaining funds to restore, compensate for, or otherwise finance recovery from the harm.

1-3.   Risk control techniques should be matched with one or more specific loss exposures because a measure taken to control one kind of risk could increase the frequency or severity of other risks by introducing new hazards.

1-4.   a.   The potential effect of having a vicious guard dog on the premises is that it will increase the liability loss exposure of a lawsuit if someone is attacked by the dog.

b.   By placing the guard dog on the premises, the increased liability loss exposure may outweigh the savings obtained from reducing the property exposures to theft and vandalism

c.   Risk control measures that may reduce property loss exposures and may not substantially increase the liability loss exposure include installing motion detectors, video surveillance cameras, or a central alarm system; hiring a human security guard; and trimming landscaping so that neighbors can better see the activities on the lot.

Educational Objective 2

2-1.   According to the domino theory, the chain of accident factors consists of the following:

- Ancestry and social environment
- Fault of person
- An unsafe act and/or a mechanical or physical hazard
- The accident itself
- The resulting injury

2-2.   H.W. Heinrich believed that the unsafe human acts comprising the third domino are far more frequent than unsafe conditions; therefore, correcting these acts is the most effective method of preventing injuries or illnesses.

2-3.   Using the general methods of control approach, control methods can be applied at the source of a hazard, along the path between the source and the exposed employee, to the employee directly, or by some combination of these.

2-4.   Five principles of risk control that follow from the technique of operations review are as follows:

    (1) An unsafe act, an unsafe condition, and an accident are all symptoms of something wrong in the management system.

    (2) Certain circumstances, unless identified and controlled, will produce severe injuries.

    (3) Safety should be managed with management setting achievable goals and planning, organizing, leading, and controlling to achieve them.

    (4) Management must specify procedures for accountability if safety efforts are to be effective.

    (5) The function of safety is to locate and define the operational errors that allow accidents to occur.

2-5.   a. The domino theory—Sam's unsafe action, reaching too far, precipitated a series of events that resulted in his injury. A number of other actions contributed to, and resulted in, Sam's awkward fall.

    b. The general methods of control approach—each element contributing to Sam's accident needs to be analyzed separately in its sequence. The contributing causes of the accident can be isolated, and the point at which the accident occurred can be identified.

    c. The energy transfer theory—as the ladder fell, the energy released Sam's weight and the upright ladder, resulting in disequilibrium.

    d. The technique of operations review (TOR) approach—the management failure that occurred was failing to designate who had the clear responsibility to substitute for the apprentice who was out sick.

    e. The system safety approach—there were several components of several systems that malfunctioned. Sam failed to perform his painting operation with good workman-like skills by overreaching. Acme failed to use good management skills in keeping adequate staffing for the overall house construction.

Educational Objective 3

3-1.   Avoidance would be an appropriate risk control technique when the expected value of losses from the activity outweighs the expected benefits of the activity.

3-2.   Loss prevention differs from other risk control techniques in the following ways:

    a. Avoidance—loss prevention does not eliminate all chance of future loss.

    b. Loss reduction—loss prevention reduces frequency without necessarily affecting loss severity, and loss reduction focuses on reducing the loss severity, not loss frequency.

3-3.   The two categories of loss reduction measures are as follows:

    (1) Pre-loss measures—applied before the loss occurs to reduce loss severity. They can also reduce loss frequency.

    (2) Post-loss measures—applied after the loss occurs to reduce the amount of property damage or number of people suffering from a single event.

▶▶

3-4.   Separation disperses a particular asset or activity over several locations and regularly relies on that asset as part of the organization's working resources. Duplication uses backups, spares, or copies of critical property, information, or capabilities and keeps them in reserve.

3-5.   a.   If the loss exposure arises from closing schools because of the cost of or lack of fuel oil, using avoidance by switching to another source of heat would be effective. However, if the loss exposure arises from lack of heat for the school regardless of the source of heat, avoidance would not be practical. Every possible source of heat can become unavailable or too expensive under some foreseeable circumstances.

b.   The school district can use several measures of loss prevention to reduce the frequency of losing government funding. One would be to purchase a year's supply of fuel oil in the summer months. Another would be to arrange for alternative, well-heated, facilities in which to hold school when fuel oil supplies are short.

c.   Loss reduction measures would be aimed at reducing severity of the loss of state and federal school funding. One option would be to lobby for a change in the funding laws to require fewer school days per year, or to allow partial funding when fewer than 180 days of school occur.

d.   The school district may be able to increase the number of independent suppliers of fuel oil so that, if one or more suppliers cannot meet the district's needs, a new supplier can provide the fuel oil during critical shortages. Much depends on the geographical scope of future fuel shortages.

Direct Your Learning

Controlling Property Loss Exposures

Educational Objectives

After learning the content of this assignment, you should be able to:

1. Explain how human characteristics, building occupancies, and the Life Safety Code affect the life safety of persons exposed to fire in buildings.

2. Describe the types of building construction, their characteristics, and how the construction affects the ability to resist fire.

3. Describe characteristics of five activities that raise special fire safety needs regarding occupancy.

4. Explain how a building's protection prevents a fire and reduces its severity once it occurs.

5. Explain how to evaluate and control hazards to a building from its exterior environment.

6. Describe mold, its effects on people, and how a risk management professional can control mold.

7. Define or describe each of the Key Words and Phrases for this assignment.

Study Materials

Required Reading:
▶ Risk Control
  • Chapter 2

Study Aids:
▶ SMART Online Practice Exams
▶ SMART Study Aids
  • Review Notes and Flash Cards— Assignment 2

Outline

- **Life Safety**
  - A. Human Characteristics
  - B. Building Occupancies
  - C. Life Safety Code
- **Construction**
  - A. Frame
  - B. Joisted Masonry
  - C. Noncombustible
  - D. Masonry Noncombustible
  - E. Modified Fire-Resistive
  - F. Fire-Resistive
  - G. Fire Divisions
- **Occupancy**
  - A. Commodity Storage
  - B. Spraying Operations
  - C. Flammable Liquids
  - D. Food Preparation
  - E. Computer Operations
- **Protection**
  - A. Fire Triangle
  - B. Ignition Sources
  - C. Internal Fire Protection
    1. Detection
    2. Suppression
  - D. External Fire Protection
  - E. Water Damage Control
  - F. Post-Fire Loss Reduction
- **Exterior Environment**
  - A. Evaluating Exterior Exposures
  - B. Controlling Exterior Exposures

- **Mold**
  - A. Description of Mold
  - B. Identification of Mold
  - C. Effects of Mold
  - D. Risk Control
    1. Loss Prevention
    2. Loss Reduction
- **Summary**
- **Appendix: Characteristics of Classes of Occupancies**

For each assignment, you should define or describe each of the Key Words and Phrases and answer each of the Review and Application Questions.

Educational Objective 1

Explain how human characteristics, building occupancies, and the Life Safety Code affect the life safety of persons exposed to fire in buildings.

Key Words and Phrases

Fire safety (p. 2.4)

Life safety (p. 2.4)

Review Questions

1-1. Distinguish fire safety from life safety. (p. 2.4)

1-2. List the twelve classes of occupancy. (p. 2.4)

1-3.   For each of the following characteristics of persons who may be the occupants of a burning building, describe how that characteristic affects the degree of hazard the person faces during a fire: (p. 2.5)

a. Age

b. Mobility

c. Awareness of the fire

d. Knowledge of the environment

e. Density (crowding)

f. Control of occupants

1-4. Explain the importance of compliance with the *Life Safety Code*. (p. 2.6)

Application Question

1-5. The Galleria is a shopping mall with a building occupancy that is primarily mercantile. However, this mall takes up an entire city block and is large enough to also include a movie theater and several bar/restaurants. The movie theater is currently showing a film that appeals to an audience under twelve years of age. At 7 PM on a Friday night, a fire occurs in the kitchen of one of the bar/restaurants. Smoke spreads rapidly through the mall causing fire alarms to go off throughout the building. Explain how the characteristics affecting building occupancies' susceptibility to fire apply to the following three groups of patrons:

a. The young children in the movie theater

b. The shoppers in clothing or department stores

c. The "happy hour" drinkers at the bar/restaurants

Educational Objective 2

Describe the types of building construction, their characteristics, and how the construction affects the ability to resist fire.

Key Words and Phrases

Frame (p. 2.7)

Joisted masonry (p. 2.7)

Heavy timber, or mill (p. 2.8)

Noncombustible (p. 2.10)

Masonry noncombustible (p. 2.10)

Modified fire-resistive (p. 2.12)

Fire-resistive (p. 2.12)

Fire division (p. 2.12)

Firewall (p. 2.12)

Fender wall (p. 2.14)

Fusible link (p. 2.14)

Review Questions

2-1. Identify the distinguishing characteristics of each of the following types of building construction:

a. Frame (p. 2.7)

b. Joisted masonry (p. 2.7)

c. Noncombustible (p. 2.10)

d. Masonry noncombustible (p. 2.10)

e. Modified fire-resistive (p. 2.12)

f. Fire-resistive (p. 2.12)

2-2. For each of the following pairs of types of building construc-
       tion, distinguish between the members of the pair in terms of
       the physical characteristics of building construction and the
       relative structural integrity of each type of construction during
       a fire:

a. Frame verses joisted masonry (pp. 2.7–2.8)

b. Joisted masonry versus masonry noncombustible
     (pp. 2.7–2.10)

c. Masonry noncombustible versus modified fire-resistive
     (pp. 2.10–2.12)

d. Modified fire-resistive versus fire-resistive (p. 2.12)

2-3. Explain the significance of the fire-resistive rating of a fire door. (p. 2.13)

Application Question

2-4. A large department store chain wants to construct a distribution center in the southern United States that will serve as a regional warehouse for a two-hundred-mile radius. Warehouse managers have informed the chain's risk management professional that under normal circumstances of staffing, availability of moving equipment, amount of inventory, and depending on where a fire originates, it will probably take one hour to evacuate 60 percent of the value of the inventory. Sixty percent is the target set by the chief financial officer, based on her level of risk tolerance. Recognizing that the cost of construction typically rises as a more fire-resistive type of construction is chosen, recommend the least expensive building construction type that will still allow the warehouse personnel to meet their 60 percent target under normal circumstances and explain why each less expensive construction type would be inappropriate.

Educational Objective 3

Describe characteristics of five activities that raise special fire safety needs regarding occupancy.

Key Word or Phrase

Multiple chimneys (p. 2.17)

Review Questions

3-1.   Briefly describe five activities that raise special fire safety needs.
       (pp. 2.14–2.21)

3-2.   Identify the risk control factors an organization should consider
       when using palletized storage. (p. 2.15)

3-3.   Identify what a risk management professional should consider
       when evaluating occupancies using flammable liquids. (p. 2.19)

3-4.   Identify what risk management professionals should focus their attention on to protect an organization's computers from fire loss. (pp. 2.21–2.22)

Application Question

3-5.   Describe the occupancies or activities that raise special fire safety needs in the following situation:

Emma has bought a fast food restaurant. She plans to store buns, wrappers, cups, bags, and other non-frozen products on storage racks and wooden pallets. Most of the products will be wrapped in plastic packaging material. Because of the limited space, the products will be stored no more than three feet apart. Every night, cleaning solvents will be used to remove the dirt and grease that accumulated during the day. These solvents will be stored next to the water heater at the back of the store room. Emma and her crew will serve mostly hamburgers and french fries. Emma's office will be behind a steel door a few feet from the front counter. In that office will be her desktop computer, which will store the records of the day's receipts. The receipts will be downloaded at the end of each day and taken home with her.

Educational Objective 4

Explain how a building's protection prevents a fire and reduces its severity once it occurs.

Key Words and Phrases

Fire triangle (p. 2.22)

Internal fire protection (p. 2.23)

External fire protection (p. 2.23)

Automatic fire suppression system (p. 2.26)

Sprinkler system (p. 2.27)

Wet-pipe system (p. 2.27)

Dry-pipe system (p. 2.28)

Deluge system (p. 2.28)

Preaction system (p. 2.28)

Water-spray system (p. 2.28)

Dry chemical system (p. 2.29)

Carbon dioxide system (p. 2.29)

Standpipe system (p. 2.31)

Review Questions

4-1. List the three required elements of a fire. (p. 2.22)

4-2. List the four classes of ignition sources sufficient to ignite fuel
      for a fire and give an example of each. (pp. 2.23–2.24)

4-3. Briefly describe the two risk control measures for internal fire
      protection. (pp. 2.24–2.25)

4-4. Identify five types of extinguishing agents used in automatic
      fire suppression systems and how a hostile fire might be extin-
      guished by each. (pp. 2.27–2.30)

4-5. Among water-based sprinkler systems, what are the distinguish-
      ing characteristics of the following: (pp. 2.27–2.28)

      a. Wet-pipe system

      b. Dry-pipe system

      c. Deluge system

      d. Preaction system

▶▶

e. Water-spray system

4-6. What factors influence the effectiveness of an organization's external fire protection? (p. 2.32)

Application Question

4-7. Removing any one of the three legs of the fire triangle can prevent or extinguish a fire. Using each of the three legs of the triangle, describe what an organization can do to prevent or extinguish a fire on its premises.

Educational Objective 5

Explain how to evaluate and control hazards to a building from its exterior environment.

Review Questions

5-1. What exterior environmental factors should a risk management professional evaluate when controlling the threat of hostile building fires? (p. 2.35)

5-2. Identify construction considerations that are important to a risk management professional when evaluating exterior exposures. (p. 2.35)

5-3. Identify the risk control measures that might be implemented to counter dangerous conditions in surrounding properties. (p. 2.36)

Application Question

5-4. Across the street from the XYZ Insurance Agency is a vacant building. The building has been vacant for over a year and the owner is considering replacing it with a gas station. Explain which occupancy of the neighboring building would create a greater hazard to the insurance agency.

Educational Objective 6

Describe mold, its effects on people, and how a risk management professional can control mold.

Review Questions

6-1. Identify a condition that must be present for mold to grow. (p. 2.37)

6-2. Identify symptoms that a risk management professional should look for that might indicate mold growth. (pp. 2.37–2.38)

6-3. For each of the following risk control techniques, describe the types of risk control measures that might be implemented to prevent losses from mold: (pp. 2.38–2.39)

a. Loss prevention

b. Loss reduction

Application Question

6-4.   A fire occurs at a grocery store. Fortunately, the building owner had installed sprinklers, which substantially reduced the severity of the fire damage. When the local fire department arrived, the fire was close to being contained and only required a small amount of additional water from their hoses to extinguish the fire completely. A few days later, the store manager noticed stained ceiling tiles, a musty odor, and black speckles on the ceiling and walls. Describe what risk control measures the store manager should implement to reduce the loss from mold.

Answers to Assignment 2 Questions

NOTE: These answers are provided to give students a basic understanding of acceptable types of responses. They often are not the only valid answers and are not intended to provide an exhaustive response to the questions.

Educational Objective 1

1-1. Fire safety refers to the risk control measures used to protect people and property from the adverse effects of hostile fires. Life safety is the portion of fire safety that focuses on the minimum building design, construction, operation, and maintenance requirements necessary to assure a safe exit from the burning portion of a building.

1-2. The twelve classes of occupancy are as follows:
   (1) Assembly
   (2) Educational
   (3) Daycare
   (4) Healthcare
   (5) Ambulatory healthcare
   (6) Detention and correctional
   (7) Residential
   (8) Residential board and care
   (9) Mercantile
   (10) Business
   (11) Industrial
   (12) Storage

1-3. The following characteristics affect the degree of hazard a building's occupants face during a fire:
   a. Age—the very old and very young have significantly higher fatality rates because they are less mobile or less aware of a fire. Therefore, the degree of hazard faced is high.
   b. Mobility—those with impaired abilities (such as those who are physically or mentally disabled, hospitalized, or incarcerated) need special attention. These factors increase the degree of hazard.
   c. Awareness of the fire—factors such as wakefulness, effects of drugs or alcohol, and activity diversions can significantly increase the degree of hazard.
   d. Knowledge of the environment—training in fire safety and evacuation procedures as well as familiarity with surroundings affect the degree of hazard.
   e. Density (crowding)—the degree of hazard increases as the density of an enclosed area increases.
   f. Control of occupants—the degree of hazard diminishes the more the occupants are subject to discipline and control.

1-4. Compliance with the *Life Safety Code* is important because of the following:

- Compliance is usually a legal requirement. Failure to comply can result in fines and other penalties.
- Lack of compliance can indicate negligence in failing to safeguard others adequately.
- Lack of compliance increases the likelihood of property, personnel, and liability losses.

1-5. a. The young children are less mobile than the general population. They may also have more difficulty understanding the purpose of the fire alarm warning and what to do when they hear it. The children may be distracted by the movie itself and may initially confuse the alarm sounds with the soundtrack of the film. If the movie is heavily attended, the density or crowding of the theater may also impede the children's ability to evacuate.

b. The shoppers in the stores are likely of all ages but most will have good mobility. Their distraction level is expected to be relatively low and they should become aware of the fire as soon as the smoke or fire alarm becomes evident. Some shoppers may be new to a store, but even if they are a repeat shopper their knowledge of the environment will not be the same as it would be if they were in their own home or place of work. Therefore, they may need assistance from an employee of the store or mall in finding the appropriate exit. Density of shoppers would likely be less than the crowded movie theater, resulting in less difficulty getting to and through an exit. However, not being young children, the shoppers may be harder to control in terms of how and where to evacuate.

c. The "happy hour" drinkers pose a unique problem. Presumably they are of drinking age and are therefore old enough to be mobile. However, depending on their state of inebriation, their mobility may be impaired and they may require special assistance to evacuate quickly. Also, because of their inebriated state, their awareness of the fire may be delayed. Their knowledge of the environment is also likely not as good as it would be if they were in their own home or place of work. The density may be less of a concern than with the young children in the theater but more of a concern than with the group of shoppers, depending on how crowded the bar/restaurants are. A unique challenge to be addressed with this group may be discipline or control of the group to keep then focused on the urgency of evacuation.

Educational Objective 2

2-1. The distinguishing characteristics of the types of building construction are as follows:

a. Frame—exterior walls are made either of combustible material (such as wood) or a noncombustible material (such as brick veneer). Wall supports, floors, and roof are made of combustible material.

b. Joisted masonry—exterior walls are made of masonry (such as brick, stone, concrete, or hollow concrete block or other noncombustible materials).

c. Noncombustible—exterior walls, floors, and roof are made of, and supported by, noncombustible materials.

d. Masonry noncombustible—exterior walls are made of masonry or of fire-resistive material with a fire-resistive rating of not less than one hour; floors and roof are made of noncombustible material with noncombustible supports.

e. Modified fire-resistive—exterior walls, floors, and roof are made of masonry or fire-resistive or other noncombustible material with a fire-resistive rating of between one and two hours.

f.   Fire-resistive—exterior walls, floors, and roof are made of masonry or other noncombustible material with a fire-resistive rating of at least two hours and a roof with a fire-resistive rating of at least one hour.

2-2.   The given pairs of types of building construction are distinguished in the following ways:

a.   Frame verses joisted masonry—in frame construction, both the walls and wall supports are made of wood; in joisted masonry, the walls are made of noncombustible, self-supporting masonry. The combustible nature of the wood makes the entire structure of the frame building susceptible to fire. For a fire of moderate intensity, the joisted masonry usually keeps the exterior walls in usable or nearly usable condition.

b.   Joisted masonry versus masonry noncombustible—in joisted masonry, the walls are noncombustible, self-supporting masonry. In a fire, the bare walls would be left standing. In masonry noncombustible, the floors and roof are made of noncombustible material, and the walls are usually made of masonry material. These buildings are generally more resistant to fire damage.

c.   Masonry noncombustible versus modified fire-resistive—modified fire-resistive provides more fire protection than masonry noncombustible because the floors and roof of the masonry noncombustible building are made of materials that do not provide as much fire protection as those in a fire-resistive building.

d.   Modified fire-resistive versus fire-resistive—in a modified fire-resistive construction, exterior walls, floors, and roof are made of masonry or fire-resistive or other noncombustible material. However, in the event of fire, fire-resistive construction provides the most fire protection.

2-3.   The fire-resistive rating of a fire door is expressed as the length of time the door is expected to hold back fire.

2-4.   The risk management professional should recommend the building construction type of modified fire-resistive. This construction type requires construction design and materials that will maintain structural integrity despite exposure to fire for between one and two hours. Although likely less expensive, frame construction is inappropriate because it has wall supports, floors, and roofs that are combustible and cannot be relied on to maintain the structural integrity needed to remove the inventory. Joisted masonry construction has noncombustible wall supports but the floors and walls are still combustible and therefore inappropriate. Noncombustible construction and masonry noncombustible may be appropriate types of construction with their exterior walls, floors, and roofs made of noncombustible materials. However, only the exterior walls (not including the floor or roof) of the masonry noncombustible type is rated for at least an hour and, as stated, one hour (time to save 60 percent of inventory) is the minimum required by the CFO. Fire-resistive construction would also provide the needed fire protection but would likely cost more to construct than masonry noncombustible and therefore are not as desirable.

Educational Objective 3

3-1.   Five activities that raise special fire safety needs are as follows:

(1)   Commodity storage—a major fire safety concern because of the concentration of value in one place and the manner in which commodities are stored.

(2)   Spraying operations—hazardous because the operation creates fine droplets of combustible fluid. Many solvents and paints are highly flammable.

(3)   Flammable liquids—potential exists for improper handling, spillage, ignition, and hazardous combinations of vapors and ignition sources.

(4) Food preparation—the accumulation of grease in hood and duct areas of cooktops, stoves, and related equipment creates a fire hazard.

(5) Computer operations—a fire loss can result in a direct loss to computer property and severe indirect consequences for the organization's operations. Hot electrical components could also short or spark in close proximity with combustible plastic, paper, and fabric in a chair or carpet.

3-2.   The risk control factors an organization should consider when using palletized storage are as follows:
- Height of storage
- Pallet construction
- Aisle spaces
- Commodity and packaging material

3-3.   A risk management professional should consider the following when evaluating occupancies using flammable liquids:
- What types of flammable liquids are used
- What amounts of flammable liquid are used in different operations
- How the flammable liquids are stored
- Where the flammable liquids are stored and used

3-4.   Risk management professionals should focus on the following to protect an organization's computers from fire loss:
- Noncombustible or fire-resistive construction of computer operations area
- Separation of computer operations area from hazardous storage or operations
- Location of computer wiring channels and air conditioning ductwork under the floor or above a dropped ceiling
- Installation of fire detection/suppression system within the computer operations area
- Interior finish and furnishings of noncombustible or of limited combustibility
- Daily removal of waste material
- Employee training in fire protection levels and emergency fire procedures

3-5.   Commodity storage is a concern. Many of the products are flammable; they are wrapped in plastic, which can cause a greater heat release, and they are stored close together, which may restrict critical access to the products when fighting a fire. Storage of flammable liquids raises concern. Cleaning solvents maybe necessary to remove the heavy grease buildup and prevent health code violations. However, storing them next to the water heater creates an unnecessarily high risk of igniting the vapors. Food preparation is another activity of concern. The grease accumulation throughout the day in the hood and duct areas of cooktops, stoves, and related equipment creates a fire hazard. Emma's computer operations are also of concern. If a fire were to destroy her office, her computer would be damaged, as would the record of her day's receipts. Because she has the prior day's receipts at home, she would only lose one day's receipts.

Educational Objective 4

4-1. The three required elements of a fire are as follows:

(1) Fuel

(2) Heat

(3) Oxygen

4-2. The four classes of ignition sufficient to ignite fuel for a fire are as follows:

(1) Chemical heat energy (oxidation)—such as smoking in an industrial premises

(2) Electrical heat energy—such as fuel flowing through a pipe releasing static electricity and igniting a fire

(3) Mechanical heat energy—such as friction between gears generating enough heat to ignite a fire

(4) Nuclear heat energy—such as if substantial amounts of nuclear fuel are used in a heating process, it could ignite from atomic particle collision

4-3. The two risk control measures for internal fire protection are as follows:

(1) Detection—devices to activate an internal fire protection system that may respond to heat, rate of temperature increase, smoke, flame, or a combination of these

(2) Suppression—measures to prevent damage or to minimize damage once a fire occurs

4-4. Five types of extinguishing agents used in automatic fire suppression systems are as follows:

(1) Water—the heat from the fire breaks or melts the sprinkler head. Water is discharged upwards or downwards and a deflector creates a spray pattern over the fire.

(2) Dry chemicals—finely divided powders in a cylinder are connected by pipes to nozzles that are positioned to distribute the powder over the fire.

(3) Carbon dioxide—stored as a liquid under pressure and discharged as a gas through pipes to the fire site.

(4) Foam—smothers the fire with a foam blanket that separates the fuel from the oxygen.

(5) Halon substitutes—extinguishes the fire by breaking the combustion chain reaction (they absorb oxygen).

4-5. Water-based sprinkler systems have the following distinguishing characteristics:

a. Wet pipe system—piping is full of water and will immediately discharge when sprinkler head opens.

b. Dry-pipe system—pipe is filled with pressurized air. When the sprinkler head opens, air pressure is released and water flows through pipes and sprinklers.

c. Deluge system—sprinkler heads remain permanently open and allow water to enter when the system is activated by a separate detection system.

d. Preaction system—same design as a deluge system except the sprinkler heads are normally closed. Both the sprinkler heads and detection components must operate before water is released.

e. Water-spray system—have either open or closed nozzles and are specifically designed for the configuration of the space being protected and the hazards in that space.

4-6.   The following factors influence the effectiveness of an organization's external fire protection:
   • Public fire hydrants are reasonable accessible
   • Hydrants have adequate water volume and pressure
   • Fire department has appropriate fire fighting equipment
   • Fire department personnel are trained and capable of responding to a fire at the facility

4-7.   Decreasing the amount of combustible material in a given area, thus controlling the fuel side of the triangle, reduces the severity of the fire. Fire-extinguishing techniques smother the flame by removing oxygen either mechanically or chemically. Removing the oxygen from a hazardous enclosed area by filling it with inert gas prevents a fire from starting. Removing the heat source will prevent ignition of the fuel.

Educational Objective 5

5-1.   The exterior environmental factors a risk management professional should evaluate when controlling the threat of hostile building fires are as follows:
   • Construction
   • Occupancy
   • Protection
   • General maintenance and housekeeping of surrounding property, which is part of its exterior environment

5-2.   Construction considerations that are important to a risk management professional when evaluating exterior exposures include the following:
   • Building materials
   • Building height and area
   • Wall openings

5-3.   Risk control measures that might be implemented to counter dangerous conditions in surrounding properties include the following:
   • Reducing the extent of wall openings facing the exposure
   • Removing combustible material from the building
   • Clearing the area between the buildings
   • Constructing a free-standing barrier between the buildings
   • Installing a water-spray system

5-4.   A vacant building presents a heightened risk because it may be a frequent shelter for vagrants and can be targets for arsonists. However, the gas station has a relatively large amount of combustible material in the form of flammable liquid stored on the premises. Ignition of the flammable liquid is not unforeseeable and the severity of damage from an ignition and resulting fire would be substantially greater than most other occupancies.

Educational Objective 6

6-1. Some form of moisture is required for mold to grow.

6-2. Symptoms that a risk management professional should look for that might indicate mold growth include the following:

- Stained ceiling tiles or walls
- Musty, earthy, or urine type odors
- Black, brown, orange, pink, or green speckles around plumbing, grout, or tile
- Mild to severe unexplained illness in combination with other building problems
- Leaky roof or flashing
- Flood or hurricane damage
- Plumbing leaks at drains and gaskets
- Lack of ventilation
- Faulty air conditioning or heating systems (HVAC)
- Cracked or disconnected hoses to kitchen appliances

6-3. a. Loss prevention measures that might be implemented to prevent losses from mold include keeping the humidity level below 50 percent, using an air conditioner or dehumidifier, using mold-inhibitors, using mold-killing products, and using air purifiers.

   b. Loss reduction measures that might be implemented to reduce losses from mold include determining if there is a mold infestation, and if so, by what type of mold; stopping the source of moisture; and drying savable material. Periodic follow-up inspections should be made after the contamination is treated.

6-4. Once the fire is out, both sources of moisture (the sprinkler system and the fire department spraying water from hoses) should have stopped. The moisture that remains should be removed and salvageable material dried. As it has been several days since the fire, and the manager has noticed an odor and visible signs of mold, samples should be taken from the areas that are suspected to contain mold. The samples should be sent to a laboratory to confirm the presence and type of mold. The type of mold will indicate which personal protective equipment (PPE) should be used. With the proper PPE, cleaning should begin by treating superficial contamination with bleach. Deeper contamination will require more aggressive treatment up to and including replacement. Once the infestation is brought under control, periodic follow-up inspections should be made to ensure no mold colonies were overlooked.

Direct Your Learning

Controlling Intellectual Property Loss Exposures

Educational Objectives

After learning the content of this assignment, you should be able to:

1. Explain what intellectual property is and how it is protected.

2. Describe the features of copyrights and risk control measures for copyright loss exposures.

3. Describe the features of trademarks and risk control measures for trademark loss exposures.

4. Describe the features of patents and risk control measures for patent loss exposures.

5. Describe the features of trade secrets and risk control measures for trade secret loss exposures.

6. Explain how intellectual property rights can overlap.

7. Define or describe each of the Key Words and Phrases for this assignment.

Study Materials

Required Reading:
▶ Risk Control
  • Chapter 3

Study Aids:
▶ SMART Online Practice Exams
▶ SMART Study Aids
  • Review Notes and Flash Cards—Assignment 3

Outline

▶ **Intellectual Property Protection**

▶ **Copyrights**
   A. Copyright Creation
   B. Copyright Ownership
   C. Copyright Duration
   D. Risk Control Measures for Copyright Loss Exposures
      1. Notice
      2. Registration
      3. Restrictive Covenants
      4. Responses to Anticipated Defenses
      5. Licensing Agreements

▶ **Trademarks**
   A. Trademark Categories
   B. Trademark Creation
   C. Trademark Duration
   D. Risk Control Measures for Trademark Loss Exposures
      1. Notice
      2. Registration
      3. Searches and Watches
      4. Licensing Agreements
      5. Restrictive Covenants
      6. Enforcement of Rights

▶ **Patents**
   A. Types of Patent
   B. Patent Creation
   C. Patent Ownership
   D. Patent Duration
   E. Risk Control Measures for Patent Loss Exposures
      1. Notice
      2. Licensing Agreements
      3. Restrictive Covenants
      4. Freedom to Operate Search

▶ **Trade Secrets**
   A. Trade Secret Creation
   B. Trade Secret Duration
   C. Risk Control Measures for Trade Secret Loss Exposures

▶ **Intellectual Property Rights Overlap**
   A. Trade Secret and Copyright
   B. Trade Secret and Patent
   C. Copyright and Patent

▶ **Summary**

Narrow the focus of what you need to learn. Remember, the Educational Objectives are the foundation of each of the Institutes' courses, and the exam is based on these Educational Objectives.

For each assignment, you should define or describe each of the Key Words and Phrases and answer each of the Review and Application Questions.

Educational Objective 1

Explain what intellectual property is and how it is protected.

Key Words and Phrases

Intellectual property (p. 3.3)

Infringement (p. 3.3)

Copyright (p. 3.4)

Trademark (p. 3.4)

Patent (p. 3.4)

Trade secret (p. 3.4)

Review Questions

1-1.   Explain why intellectual property is important to a risk management professional. (p. 3.3)

1-2. Briefly describe the four common types of protection for intellectual property. (p. 3.4)

1-3. Describe how intellectual property is protected in the following locations: (p. 3.5)

a. United States

b. Internationally

Application Question

1-4. After years of expensive research, the engineers at Acme Corporation have developed a new microchip that is half the size and twice as fast as any other available chip. Acme would like to prevent its competitors from copying its chip and selling it as their own. Explain which of the four intellectual property protections may help Acme.

Educational Objective 2

Describe the features of copyrights and risk control measures for copyright infringement loss exposures.

Key Words and Phrases

Work for hire (p. 3.6)

Published (p. 3.7)

Laches (p. 3.9)

Review Questions

2-1.   Identify the important features of a copyright. (p. 3.6)

2-2.   Identify the three criteria required for copyright creation.
       (p. 3.6)

2-3.   Describe risk control measures that can be used for copyright
       loss exposures. (pp. 3.7–3.10)

2-4.   Explain why copyright owners place copyright notices on their published works and describe the notice methods commonly used for published and Internet materials. (p. 3.8)

Application Question

2-5.   Sarah has worked as a human resource specialist at a local college for ten years. During that time she was asked to draft several amendments to the college's employee handbook regarding prevention of workplace injuries, including workplace violence. Sarah has decided to switch jobs and work for a local hospital. She has told her former supervisor in her exit interview that because she wrote the amendments she feels she has a right to use them at her new job. Do you agree? Why or why not?

Educational Objective 3
Describe the features of trademarks and risk control measures for trademark loss exposures.

Key Words and Phrases
Servicemark (p. 3.10)

Trade dress (p. 3.10)

Review Questions

3-1. Explain how an organization would use a trademark to protect its intellectual property. (p. 3.10)

3-2. Distinguish between the following: (p. 3.10)

a. Trademark

b. Servicemark

c. Trade dress

3-3. Describe the categories of trademarks. (p. 3.11)

3-4. Which types of trademarks are not protected by federal statutes? (p. 3.11)

3-5. Identify two requirements in the creation of a trademark. (pp. 3.11–3.12)

3-6. Describe risk control measures used to protect an organization's trademarks and servicemarks. (pp. 3.13–3.14)

Application Question

3-7. George is a risk management professional who is employed by an ice cream producer. Every year the producer would introduce a new flavor to the public and refer to the new flavor by a new trademark name. George registered the trademarks with the USPTO as each of the new flavors was introduced. Now, after 9 years, what should George be concerned about to retain the trademark protection?

Educational Objective 4

Describe the features of patents and risk control measures for patent loss exposures.

Key Words and Phrases

Utility patent (p. 3.15)

Design patent (p. 3.15)

Plant patent (p. 3.15)

Review Questions

4-1. Describe the important features of a patent. (pp. 3.15–3.17)

4-2. Identify the criteria required for U.S. patent eligibility. (p. 3.16)

4-3. Describe how the following risk control measures protect an organization's patents: (pp. 3.18–3.19)

a. Notice

b. Licensing agreements

c. Restrictive covenants

d. Freedom to operate search

Application Question

4-4. Alpha, a motorcycle manufacturer, has developed a wider and
longer front suspension system that is considered new and
innovative. In addition, industry analysts predict buyers will
find the motorcycle's new design to be more aesthetically pleasing than the design of any of its competitors, which was the
intent of the designers. A surprising unintended benefit is that
road tests have proved the new design to also be more stable.
What type of patents can Alpha apply for and would it make
a difference if its sales department predicts it needs seventeen
years without a similar design from its competitors to break-
even on Alpha's research and development costs?

Educational Objective 5
Describe the features of trade secrets and risk control measures for trade secret loss exposures.

Key Word or Phrase
Reverse engineering (p. 3.19)

Review Questions

5-1.   Identify two loss exposures associated with trade secrets.
(p. 3.20)

5-2.   Explain how courts determine trade secret status. (p. 3.20)

5-3.   Identify risk control measures that can be used to protect trade
secrets. (p. 3.21)

Application Question

5-4. A computer hacker extracted the secret recipe of a soft drink manufacturer's best-selling soft drink and then anonymously e-mailed the recipe to the manufacturer's competitors. The hacker was able to remain unidentified. Can the competitors use the recipe?

Educational Objective 6

Explain how intellectual property rights can overlap.

Review Questions

6-1. Explain how intellectual property rights change through publication. (p. 3.22)

6-2. Explain why an organization might choose to maintain an invention as a trade secret rather than pursue a patent. (p. 3.22)

6-3. Describe the difference in protection provided by copyright and patent. (p. 3.22)

Application Question

6-4. If a descendant of President Abraham Lincoln has possession of memoirs of the president that are unknown to anyone else, what two potentially overlapping intellectual property protections can the descendant use?

Answers to Assignment 3 Questions

NOTE: These answers are provided to give students a basic understanding of acceptable types of responses. They often are not the only valid answers and are not intended to provide an exhaustive response to the questions.

Educational Objective 1

1-1. Intellectual property is important to a risk management professional for the following reasons:
- Organizations may not have an accurate inventory of what intellectual property they already own.
- Organizations face liability loss exposures if they inadvertently infringe the intellectual property rights of others.

1-2. The four common types of protection for intellectual property are as follows:
   (1) Copyright—the right to exclusively own and control an original written document, piece of music, software, or other form of expression
   (2) Trademark—the right to exclusively own and control a distinctive design or set of words that legally identifies a product or service as belonging to an organization
   (3) Patent—for a limited period provides the right to exclusively own and control a new, useful, and nonobvious invention
   (4) Trade secret—protection of a practice, method, process, design, or other information used confidentially by an organization to maintain a competitive advantage

1-3. Intellectual property is protected in the following ways:
   a. United States—laws (including statutes, regulations, and case law) that help to define who the owners of intellectual property are and what rights accrue to those owners.
   b. Internationally—most countries offer reciprocal rights of protection; notable exceptions being Thailand, Taiwan, and Malaysia. Treaties regarding international intellectual property rights include the Berne Convention (copyrights), the Patent Cooperation Treaty (patents), the Paris Convention (patents and trademarks), and the General Agreement on Tariffs and Trade (GATT) (trade secrets).

1-4. Both patent and trade secret protection may help Acme. A patent may be available for such a new, useful, and nonobvious invention. A patent would allow Acme to exclusively own and control, for a limited time, what it has spent so much to invent. Trade secret protection is available if Acme does not want to disclose the chip's design or how it is manufactured. An additional benefit of a trade secret is that it can last indefinitely. However, the technology for computer chips changes so rapidly that this particular benefit may not be of much value to Acme.

Educational Objective 2

2-1. The important features of a copyright are as follows:
- Copyright creation
- Copyright ownership
- Copyright duration

2-2. The three criteria required for copyright creation are as follows:

(1) The work must be original

(2) The work must be fixed in a tangible medium of expression that is permanently recorded

(3) The work must have some degree of creativity

2-3. Risk control measures that can be used for copyright loss exposures are as follows:

- Notice—a © symbol, the year, and the copyright owner's name are placed or embedded on published work so that infringing parties cannot claim lack of knowledge of copyright.

- Registration—provides evidence of ownership and potential for significant monetary damages. The work is registered with the U.S. Copyright Office by filing a form, two samples of the published work, and a fee.

- Restrictive covenants—a legally binding contract that, on termination of employment or contract, restricts the post-termination activities. It provides additional protection to reduce the likelihood of copyright infringement.

- Responses to anticipated defenses—potential responses to counter common infringement defenses.

- Licensing agreements—copyright owners can grant permission to others to use their copyrighted materials.

2-4. Owners provide copyright notice for published and internet materials to reduce copyright infringement losses and to make it easier to collect damages from parties who copy the work without permission. Notice methods include the following:

- Published—symbol ©, followed by the year published, and the name of the copyright owner

- Internet—digital watermarking that embeds information about the copyright owner into the video, audio, or graphics files

2-5. No, she does not have the right to use the amendments at her new job without the consent of her former employer. Her writing was a work for hire, which means that her employer owns the copyright. The college may also have had her sign a restrictive covenant, which is a legally binding agreement that would give the college the right to prevent Sarah from using the amendments she drafted.

Educational Objective 3

3-1. An organization would use a trademark (a distinctive word, phrase, logo, or other marketing device) in the hope that the customer will relate it to the organization's reputation for quality and to prevent customers from confusing its products with its competitors' products.

3-2. a. Trademark—a mark that is used to distinguish an organization's products from its competitors' products. It can be a distinctive word, phrase, logo, or other marketing device.

b. Servicemark—a mark that is used to distinguish an organization's services from those of its competition.

c. Trade dress—the total image of a product or service (such as unique packaging) that distinguishes it from its competition in the marketplace.

3-3.   The categories of trademarks are as follows:
- Arbitrary mark—word or phrase that appears to have been used randomly
- Fanciful mark—word or phrase that conjures up an image that is imaginative
- Suggestive mark—word or phrase that implies certain product qualities
- Descriptive mark—word or phrase that describes the product

3-4.   Trademarks that are not protected by federal statutes include the following:
- Generic trademarks that describe the type of product rather than the brand
- People's names, other than names that become well known through use or advertising, such as McDonald's
- Trade names or the name of a business unless the name is used in the marketplace to identify the product produced by the business

3-5.   Two requirements in the creation of a trademark are as follows:
   (1) The mark must be distinctive; that is, a unique symbol or logo, a fabricated word, a word that is unexpected in the context it is used, a word that creates a fanciful image, or a word that describes a product's qualities.
   (2) The trademark's owner must be the first to introduce the mark into the stream of commerce. This is accomplished by attaching the trademark to a product being sold or using it in product marketing.

3-6.   Risk control measures used to protect an organization's trademarks and servicemarks are as follows:
- Notice—register the trademarks, servicemarks, logos, domain names, and graphics with the United States Patent and Trademark Office (USPTO) and designate with ™ or ® as appropriate
- Registration—register the mark with the USPTO
- Searches and watches—determine if anyone else has a similar mark
- Licensing agreements—prepare before allowing anyone else to use an organization's mark to address quality control issues and to limit liability if the licensee fails to meet quality standards
- Restrictive covenants—provide additional trademark protection because, through agreement, parties promise not to infringe
- Enforcement of rights—cease-and-desist letters, notification of intent to sue, and filing oppositions with the USPTO help organizations deal with infringers

3-7.   The duration of a trademark that is registered with the USPTO is ten years. However, the registration can be renewed indefinitely provided it is renewed every ten years. Therefore, George should set up a diary system to remind him to renew each of the trademark registrations prior to its ten-year anniversary. As the producer has been in business for nine years, presumably it has nine flavors being sold to the public under nine trademark names. The first flavor, which was introduced nine years ago, must have its trademark registration renewed soon.

Educational Objective 4

4-1. The important features of a patent are as follows:

- Patent types—types include utility, design, or plant patent.
- Patent creation—patent must be applied for and approved by the USPTO. Inventors may apply to countries individually or file an international application. The invention enters the public domain if the application is rejected or if the patent has expired.
- Patent ownership—patent inventor owns the patent rights but may assign rights to another party.
- Patent duration—patent durations vary from fourteen to twenty years depending on the type of patent.

4-2. To be eligible to receive a U.S. patent, an invention must be the following:

- New
- Useful
- Nonobvious

4-3. The risk control measures that protect an organization's patents are as follows:

a. Notice—marking a product with "patent pending" or a patent number provides a presumption of notice and prevents claims of unintentional infringement.

b. Licensing agreements—transfer the risk of infringement claims to the licensee.

c. Restrictive covenants—"work for hire" or "hire to invent" employment contracts and confidentiality agreements clarify employee rights to intellectual property.

d. Freedom to operate search—helps protect against patent infringement allegations against the organization.

4-4. Alpha could apply for a utility patent or a design patent. A utility patent is possible since the new motorcycle is more stable, which makes the new design useful beyond aesthetics. However, Alpha could also be granted a design patent since the new motorcycle's design was intended to be and is considered aesthetically pleasing. A utility patent has a duration of twenty years while a design patent lasts only fourteen years. Since the sales department has advised that it needs seventeen years to break even, and logically the sales department would want as long a period as possible before the competition matches its product, Alpha should apply for a utility patent.

Educational Objective 5

5-1. Two loss exposures associated with trade secrets are as follows:

(1) Someone else might honestly create the same invention, process, or method and get it patented.

(2) The trade secret might be stolen or disclosed as a result of negligence.

5-2. Courts determine trade secret status by investigating the following:

- How widespread is knowledge about the secret outside of the business?
- How much of the secret is disclosed to the business's employees?
- What steps are taken to guard the secret?
- What is the secret's commercial value?
- How hard is it for someone to acquire or duplicate the secret?

5-3. Risk control measures that can be used to protect trade secrets include the following:
- Disclose information to employees on a need-to-know basis only
- Require security measures to gain access to the area where secret information is used or maintained
- Control documentation regarding the secret
- Require employees to sign a restrictive covenant

5-4. If the manufacturer can convince the court that it used reasonable safeguards to protect the recipe and was not negligent in allowing the release of this information, it should be able to rely on trade secret protection to prevent use of the recipe and further distribution of the recipe.

Educational Objective 6

6-1. Publication is not required to create copyright protection, as it automatically applies to any work of expression when it becomes fixed in a tangible medium of expression. However, once published, trade secret protection is lost.

6-2. An organization might choose to maintain an invention as a trade secret rather than pursue a patent because of the following:
- Full disclosure is required for an issued patent
- Trade secrets can be maintained indefinitely

6-3. The difference in protection provided by copyright and patent is that copyright protects the expression of an idea but not the idea itself, whereas a patent protects the idea itself but not how the idea is expressed.

6-4. When the memoirs were first written, both copyright and trade secret protections applied. However, these memoirs must have been written over one hundred years ago, during which time the copyright protection would have expired. Trade secret protection can continue indefinitely, so potentially it is still a viable protection today.

Direct Your Learning

Controlling Criminal Loss Exposures

Educational Objectives

After learning the content of this assignment, you should be able to:

1. Describe the distinctive features of criminal loss exposures and their implications for risk management.

2. Describe the characteristics of common crimes.

3. Explain why, when, and how an organization should use risk control measures to reduce the *frequency* of its crime losses.

4. Explain why, when, and how an organization should use risk control measures to reduce the *severity* of its crime losses.

5. Explain why crime risk models are useful in projecting the occurrence of future crimes.

6. Define or describe each of the Key Words and Phrases for this assignment.

Study Materials

Required Reading:
▶ Risk Control
• Chapter 4

Study Aids:
▶ SMART Online Practice Exams
▶ SMART Study Aids
• Review Notes and Flash Cards— Assignment 4

Outline

▶ **Distinctive Features**
  A. Hostile Intent
  B. Continual Evaluation of Risk Control Efforts

▶ **Characteristics of Common Crimes**
  A. Burglary
  B. Robbery
  C. Shoplifting
  D. Fraud
  E. Embezzlement
  F. Forgery and Counterfeiting
  G. Vandalism
  H. Arson
  I. Terrorism
  J. Espionage
  K. Computer Crime
    1. Computer Sabotage
    2. Fraud and Embezzlement
    3. Computer Network Breach
    4. Theft Through Hacking
    5. Theft of Data Storage Systems
    6. Denial of Service and Theft of Computer Time
    7. Espionage

▶ **Risk Control Measures**
  A. Institute Sound Personnel Policies
  B. Institute Physical Controls
    1. Alarms
    2. Watchmen
    3. Surveillance Cameras
    4. Locks, Bars, and Safes
  C. Institute Computer Controls
  D. Institute Procedural Controls
  E. Institute Managerial Controls
    1. Education
    2. Applicant Screening
    3. Rotation of Employees
  F. Investigate and Prosecute Crimes
  G. Reduce Scale of Crime
  H. Implement Post-Crime Rapid Recovery

▶ **Crime Risk Models**

▶ **Summary**

▶ **Appendix A: Representative Risk Control Measures Against Burglary**

▶ **Appendix B: Representative Risk Control Measures Against Robbery**

▶ **Appendix C: Representative Risk Control Measures Against Shoplifting**

▶ **Appendix D: Representative Risk Control Measures Against Fraud**

▶ **Appendix E: Representative Risk Control Measures Against Embezzlement**

▶ **Appendix F: Representative Risk Control Measures Against Counterfeiting/Forgery**

▶ **Appendix G: Representative Risk Control Measures Against Vandalism**

▶ **Appendix H: Representative Risk Control Measures Against Arson**

▶ **Appendix I: Representative Risk Control Measures Against Terrorism**

▶ **Appendix J: Representative Risk Control Measures Against Espionage**

▶ **Appendix K: Representative Risk Control Measures Against Computer Crime**

For each assignment, you should define or describe each of the Key Words and Phrases and answer each of the Review and Application Questions.

Educational Objective 1

Describe the distinctive features of criminal loss exposures and their implications for risk management.

Review Questions

1-1. Describe the distinctive features of criminal loss exposures. (pp. 4.3–4.4)

1-2. What may organizations have that present opportunities for crime? (p. 4.4)

1-3. Identify risk control measures that focus on eliminating weaknesses that make an organization a relatively easy crime target. (p. 4.5)

Application Question

1-4. Concerned about the accumulation of highly combustible paper trash, Sam, the building supervisor for a thirty-story office building, made sure the cleaning crew hauled the trash away at the end of their late night shift. However, a large accumulation of trash was usually present from 9:30 PM until 10 PM when the cleaning crew hauled it away. How might knowledge of the cleaning crew's procedures affect the fire loss exposure of the building and its inhabitants?

Educational Objective 2

Describe the characteristics of common crimes.

Key Words and Phrases

Burglary (p. 4.6)

Robbery (p. 4.7)

Shoplifting (p. 4.7)

Fraud (p. 4.8)

Embezzlement (p. 4.8)

Forgery (p. 4.9)

Counterfeiting (p. 4.9)

Vandalism (p. 4.9)

Arson (p. 4.9)

Terrorism (p. 4.10)

Espionage (p. 4.10)

Computer crime (p. 4.11)

Computer sabotage (p. 4.11)

Review Questions

2-1.   Identify characteristics of common crimes. (p. 4.5)

2-2. Describe the potential punishments imposed by criminal and civil courts (p. 4.5)

2-3. Describe each of the following crimes against property that a risk management professional needs to consider in controlling crime risk: (pp. 4.6–4.9)

a. Burglary

b. Robbery

c. Shoplifting

d. Fraud

▶▶

e. Embezzlement

f. Forgery and counterfeiting

2-4. Describe the appropriate focus of risk control measures for each of the crimes listed in the previous question. (pp. 4.7–4.10)

Application Question

2-5. George is responsible for information system security for his organization, which stores the names, social security numbers, dates of birth, and other account information on its customers. Describe two criminal acts against his organization's computer system that George should anticipate and briefly describe risk control measures that can prevent or reduce the loss from these criminal acts.

Educational Objective 3

Explain why, when, and how an organization should use risk control measures to reduce the *frequency* of its crime losses.

Key Word or Phrase

Perimeter system (p. 4.18)

Review Questions

3-1.   Identify risk control measures that focus on deterrence and detection. (p. 4.16)

3-2.   Identify physical controls that might reduce criminal opportunities and prevent crime loss. (p. 4.17)

3-3.   Briefly describe how the following physical controls might reduce theft losses: (pp. 4.18–4.20)

   a. Alarms

b. Watchmen

c. Surveillance cameras

d. Locks, bars, and safes

3-4. Describe risk controls that might control access to computer
      facilities, software, and output in the following situations:
      (pp. 4.21–4.22)

      a. When the facility is not in use

      b. When the facility is in use

3-5.   Describe managerial controls used to reduce criminal opportunity. (p. 4.25)

Application Question

3-6.   Fresh Grocery Store has experienced a sharp increase in inventory shrinkage. The store manager suspects employee theft. What personnel policies can the store's risk management professional implement to prevent or reduce the loss from this crime?

Educational Objective 4

Explain why, when, and how an organization should use risk control measures to reduce the *severity* of its crime losses.

Review Questions

4-1.   Identify three layers of defense against a criminal attack that can reduce the scale of crime. (p. 4.28)

4-2.   Describe possible methods of personnel verification. (p. 4.28)

4-3. Identify post-crime recovery measures that aid in loss reduction. (p. 4.28)

Application Question

4-4. Larry operates a jewelry store in local mall. He knows that he is a target for burglary and robbery because he sells items of high value that are easily transportable. Describe the alarm systems Larry may consider.

Educational Objective 5

Explain why crime risk models are useful in projecting the occurrence of future crimes.

Review Questions

5-1. Why might a risk management professional use a crime risk model to forecast criminal behavior? (p. 4.28)

5-2. Describe an event tree and how it is used by a risk management professional to model crime risks. (p. 4.29)

5-3.   Describe the limitations of using crime risk models to control crime losses. (p. 4.29)

Application Question

5-4.   A terrorist cell in a large domestic city has developed the intent and logistic capability to attack a local financial institution. As a risk manager for this institution, you have decided to consult with an expert to create an event tree to assess this potential threat. Describe the branches you would expect the expert to use.

Answers to Assignment 4 Questions

NOTE: These answers are provided to give students a basic understanding of acceptable types of responses. They often are not the only valid answers and are not intended to provide an exhaustive response to the questions.

Educational Objective 1

1-1. The distinctive features of criminal loss exposures are as follows:

- Hostile intent—crime is an intentional act; therefore, to reduce crime frequency and severity, or to improve the predictability of crime losses, risk control must focus on hostile intent.
- Continual evaluation of risk control efforts—criminals discover weaknesses in an organization's processes; therefore, organizations must continually evaluate risk control efforts.

1-2. Organizations might have the following that present opportunities for crime:

- High-value
- Easily transported items
- Unguarded property
- Vulnerable people
- Unprotected key operations

1-3. Risk control measures that focus on eliminating weaknesses that make an organization a relatively easy crime target include the following:

- Shielding the organization's assets and activities by maintaining physical, procedural, and managerial barriers that reduce criminal opportunities
- Reducing criminals' perceptions that crimes can be committed without detection and punishment

1-4. An arsonist with hostile intent could use this knowledge to direct an ignition source to this large accumulation of highly combustible trash between 9:30 PM and 10 PM, causing fire damage to the building. The fact the cleaning crew is in the building at that time presents an additional loss exposure because their lives would be endangered.

Educational Objective 2

2-1. Characteristics of common crimes include acts that violate the peace and order of the general population, acts that are also torts against crime victims, and acts that are defined either by common law precedents or by statutes.

2-2. Punishments from criminal courts can include fines, imprisonment, loss of some civil rights (such as to serve in public office or to vote), or other penalties. Punishments from civil courts can include monetary damages or other legal remedies.

2-3. A risk management professional needs to consider how an organization's property may be damaged, lost, or compromised by each of the following:

a. Burglary—breaking into or out of a closed building or space not open for business to commit a felony

b.   Robbery—taking tangible personal property from another person by force or by threat of force against that person or against another

c.   Shoplifting—removing merchandise from a store by stealth without purchasing it

d.   Fraud—using deception to induce another to act to his or her detriment

e.   Embezzlement—fraudulent taking of money or other personal property by the person to whom that property has been entrusted

f.   Forgery and counterfeiting—creating false documents, creating artwork as genuine, or duplicating a country's currency

2-4.   Risk control measures for the given crimes should focus on the following:

- Burglary—protecting boundaries or perimeters of a building or an area
- Robbery—protecting the safety of personnel and customers
- Shoplifting—establishing security procedures and surveillance systems to detect theft, and on-site procedures for handling suspected thieves
- Fraud—identifying dishonest persons, detecting fraud promptly, and pressing vigorously for civil and criminal legal sanctions against those who commit fraud
- Embezzlement—performing employee background checks on potential employees, enforcing the organization's procedures, and promptly addressing violated procedures
- Forgery and counterfeiting—verifying the authenticity of currency, documents, or other items the organization accepts in exchange for the values it provides, and controlling access and use of all the organization's documents

2-5.   George should anticipate his organization's computer system being attached by computer network breach and/or theft through hacking. Appropriate risk control measures for computer network breach include assigning individuals to specific terminals and programs and limiting computer access to authorized persons who use a personal code, password, or physical identifier and password. Risk control measures for theft through hacking include using firewalls, using security antivirus software, and hiring computer experts.

Educational Objective 3

3-1.   Risk control measures that focus on deterrence and detection include the following:

- Instituting sound personnel policies
- Instituting physical controls
- Instituting computer controls
- Instituting procedural controls
- Instituting managerial controls
- Investigating and prosecuting crimes

3-2.   Physical controls that might reduce criminal opportunities and prevent crime loss include the following:

- Placing tangible barriers between would-be criminals and their targets
- Placing a crucial or vulnerable facility in a remote location
- Conducting sensitive activities near the center of an organization's facility
- Surrounding vulnerable property with intense lighting

3-3.   Physical controls that might reduce theft losses include the following:

a.   Alarms—detect intruders who have already entered the premises

b.   Watchmen—perform periodic patrols to ensure that the building structure and its contents are secure from fire, burglary, vandalism, and terrorism

c.   Surveillance cameras—photograph criminals in the process of committing a crime

d.   Locks, bars, and safes—restrict entry

3-4.   Access to computer facilities, software, and output might be controlled in the following ways:

a.   By doing the following when the facility is not in use:

- Securely locking the entrance and all other openings

- Constructing walls, ceilings, doors, and floors so that surreptitious entry is difficult

- Installing a proper security system

b.   By doing the following when the facility is in use:

- Securely locking the entrance and all other openings

- Monitoring the building entrance and keeping a log of those who enter and leave

- Maintaining a current list of personnel authorized to enter

- Controlling access to areas within the facility

- Establishing a storage library and implementing access controls to protect it

- Establishing distinctions of authority and responsibility

- Building controls directly into software programs

3-5.   Managerial controls used to reduce criminal opportunity include the following:

- Education—provide each employee with a full explanation of the purposes and extent of crime risk control

- Applicant screening—hire and retain a reasonably suitable, trustworthy, and competent work force

- Rotation of employees—change job assignments, locations, or routes

3-6.   The risk management professional should implement a personnel policy that requires background checks on potential employees, treats all employees fairly, resolves grievances promptly and equitably, and terminates or specifies other appropriate actions against employees who steal from the store. To implement these risk control measures, the risk management professional must work closely with human resources personnel because of the legal limitations imposed on organizations doing employee background checks.

Educational Objective 4

4-1.   Three layers of defense against a criminal attack that can reduce the scale of crime are as follows:

(1) Physical

(2) Human

(3) Computer-based

4-2.   Methods of personnel verification might include identity photographs and signatures, or capturing biomedical information such as fingerprints or eye scans.

4-3.   Post-crime recovery measures that aid in loss reduction include the following:
   • Full back-up computer systems at an independent location
   • Contingency plans
   • Storage of vital legal and technical documents in a secure, fire-proof off-site repository

4-4.   Alarm systems do not prevent burglars from entering a building or property but they might help an organization reduce the severity of crime losses by detecting the intruder. Larry may consider the following types of alarm systems to help the jewelry store reduce crime losses from theft:

   a.   Perimeter system—opening a door or window interrupts the electrical current and activates an alarm
   b.   Local alarm system—buttons or foot pedals can send an alarm to interior or exterior alarms
   c.   Central alarm system—buttons or foot pedals can send a silent alarm to a central location or to the police

Educational Objective 5

5-1.   A risk management professional might use a crime risk model to forecast criminal behavior because the projections indicate an efficient anti-crime resource allocation and provide crime underwriting and insurance risk management.

5-2.   An event tree is a sequence of possible events that might lead to a crime loss. Each event constitutes a branch in the event tree. A risk management professional determines overall frequency and severity of loss by considering the range of alternative loss-generating scenarios and associating each scenario with the likelihood of occurrence.

5-3.   Limitations of using crime risk models to control crime losses include the following:
   • Limited availability of actual risk experience against which models can be validated
   • Cost of developing the models
   • Skill required to program the models and interpret their results

5-4.   To create an event tree to assess this potential threat, the expert would likely use the following branches:
   • The terrorist's choice of weapon—are there historical data to suggest a level of expertise and preference in employing certain weapons?
   • The terrorist's choice of target—destruction of or damage to which target, if successfully attacked, will best serve the terrorist's goal?
   • Level of attack success—how soft is the target in terms of being unable to prevent or reduce the damages from an attack by the terrorist's weapon of choice?
   • Size of the loss—how great an economic loss is required for the attack to be perceived as a success by the terrorist?

Don't spend time on material you have already mastered. The SMART Review Notes are organized by the Educational Objectives found in each course guide assignment to help you track your study.

Direct Your Learning

Understanding Disaster Recovery Plans for Natural Disasters

Educational Objectives

After learning the content of this assignment, you should be able to:

1. Describe the following fundamental concepts of disaster recovery planning:

    *   Definition of a disaster

    *   Phases of a disaster

    *   Goals of disaster recovery

    *   Key considerations for disaster recovery

2. Describe the purpose of, focus of, procedures for, and key elements of a disaster recovery plan.

3. Describe the nature of and the pre-loss and post-loss actions appropriate for temperature extremes causes of loss.

4. Describe the nature of and the pre-loss and post-loss actions appropriate for wind causes of loss.

5. Describe the nature of and the pre-loss and post-loss actions appropriate for water causes of loss.

6. Describe the nature of and the pre-loss and post-loss actions appropriate for land causes of loss.

7. Describe the nature of and the pre-loss and post-loss actions appropriate for other property causes of loss.

8. Describe the shutdown procedures that are appropriate after a disaster.

9. Define or describe each of the Key Words and Phrases for this assignment.

Outline

▶ **Fundamental Concepts**

A. Definition of a Disaster

B. Phases of a Disaster

C. Goals of Disaster Recovery

1. Pre-Loss Goals

2. Post-Loss Goals

D. Key Considerations for Disaster Recovery

1. Causes of Loss of Disasters

2. Length of Warning Time for Disasters

3. Pre-Loss and Post-Loss Actions for Disasters

▶ **Disaster Recovery Plans**

A. Purpose

B. Focus

1. Loss Prevention

2. Loss Reduction

3. Disaster Recovery Coordination

4. Post-Disaster Recovery Actions

C. Procedures

D. Key Elements

1. Organizational Structure

2. Personnel

3. Production Facilities

4. Operating Funds

5. Market Standing

▶ **Disaster Recovery for Temperature Extremes Causes of Loss**

A. Fire and Explosion

1. Pre-Loss Actions

2. Post-Loss Actions

B. Severe Cold Weather

1. Pre-Loss Actions

2. Post-Loss Actions

▶ **Disaster Recovery for Wind Causes of Loss**

A. Windstorm

1. Pre-Loss Actions

2. Post-Loss Actions

B. Tornado

1. Pre-Loss Actions

2. Post-Loss Actions

▶ **Disaster Recovery for Water Causes of Loss**

A. Flood

1. Pre-Loss Actions

2. Post-Loss Actions

B. Hurricane

1. Pre-Loss Actions

2. Post-Loss Actions

C. Hailstorm

1. Pre-Loss Actions

2. Post-Loss Actions

D. Snowstorm

1. Pre-Loss Actions

2. Post-Loss Actions

E. Ice Storm

1. Pre-Loss Actions

2. Post-Loss Actions

F. Avalanche

▶ **Disaster Recovery for Land Causes of Loss**

A. Earthquake

1. Pre-Loss Actions

2. Post-Loss Actions

B. Landslide or Mudslide

1. Pre-Loss Actions

2. Post-Loss Actions

C. Blasting

1. Pre-Loss Actions

2. Post-Loss Actions

D. Mining

E. Sinkhole

F. Soil Deterioration

1. Pre-Loss Actions

2. Post-Loss Actions

G. Volcanic Action

▶ **Disaster Recovery for Other Property Causes of Loss**
   A. Thunderstorm
      1. Pre-Loss Actions
      2. Post-Loss Actions
   B. Collapse
      1. Pre-Loss Actions
      2. Post-Loss Actions
   C. Hazardous Material
      1. Pre-Loss Actions
      2. Post-Loss Actions
▶ **Shutdown Procedures**
▶ **Summary**

Reduce the number of Key Words and Phrases that you must review. SMART Flash Cards contain the Key Words and Phrases and their definitions, allowing you to set aside those cards that you have mastered.

For each assignment, you should define or describe each of the Key Words and Phrases and answer each of the Review and Application Questions.

Educational Objective 1

Describe the following fundamental concepts of disaster recovery planning:

- Definition of a disaster
- Phases of a disaster
- Goals of disaster recovery
- Key considerations for disaster recovery

Key Word or Phrase

Disaster (p. 5.4)

Review Questions

1-1.   Identify the four fundamental concepts of disaster recovery and how a risk management professional effectively applies these concepts. (pp. 5.4–5.6)

1-2.   Briefly describe the four phases of a disaster. (pp. 5.4–5.5)

1-3.   Identify the four pre-loss goals of disaster recovery. (p. 5.5)

1-4.   Identify six post-loss goals of disaster recovery. (p. 5.5)

1-5.   Identify the three key considerations of disaster recovery. (p. 5.6)

1-6.   Identify the three general categories of causes of loss of disasters. (p. 5.6)

Application Question

1-7.   A manufacturer's risk management professional is concerned with causes of loss that may result in a disaster. Which categories of causes of loss deserve most of the risk management professional's attention and why?

Educational Objective 2

Describe the purpose of, focus of, procedures for, and key elements of a disaster recovery plan.

Key Word or Phrase

Catastrophe model (p. 5.9)

Review Questions

2-1.   What should a risk management professional take account of when developing a disaster recovery plan? (p. 5.8)

2-2.   Identify what should be included in an effective disaster recovery planning process. (p. 5.8)

2-3.   Identify the major areas addressed by effective disaster recovery. (p. 5.8)

2-4. Identify the factors used by catastrophe models to generate projections. (p. 5.10)

2-5. Explain how an organization might tailor a disaster response to a disaster situation. (pp. 5.11–5.12)

2-6. Identify the key elements that should be safeguarded during an emergency to restore normal operations after a disaster. (p. 5.12)

2-7. Describe the information that is generally included in a written disaster recovery procedures manual. (p. 5.13)

2-8. Identify characteristics that people appointed to a crisis management team should possess. (p. 5.14)

2-9.   Explain why an organization's disaster recovery plan should implement the following elements: (pp. 5.17–5.19)

   a. Production facilities

   b. Operating funds

   c. Market standing

Application Question

2-10. Pharmaceutical Manufacturer's risk management professional is concerned that the company's market standing will falter following a disaster and thereby create a larger disaster. Who are the parties that Pharmaceutical Manufacturer needs to reassure and what assurance should be given to them?

Educational Objective 3

Describe the nature of and the pre-loss and post-loss actions appropriate for temperature extremes causes of loss.

Key Word or Phrase

Wind chill index (p. 5.21)

Review Questions

3-1.   Explain why an organization should establish a disaster recovery plan to handle temperature extremes causes of loss. (p. 5.20)

3-2.   Explain why a disaster recovery plan created for fire and explosion should focus on pre-loss actions and identify the types of pre-loss measures that are typically included in such a plan. (p. 5.20)

3-3.   Explain why the wind chill index is considered to be a better indicator than temperature alone. (p. 5.21)

Application Question

3-4. Mexico Distributor is having a warehouse built in Canada so that it can better serve its customers. Identify building design features that may be needed in the Canadian warehouse that do not exist in the Mexican warehouse.

Educational Objective 4

Describe the nature of and the pre-loss and post-loss actions appropriate for wind causes of loss.

Key Word or Phrase

Windstorm (p. 5.23)

Review Questions

4-1. Identify pre-loss actions in a disaster recovery plan for windstorm causes of loss. (p. 5.25)

4-2. List the characteristics exhibited by tornadoes. (p. 5.25)

4-3. Explain why predicting the occurrence of tornadoes is difficult. (p. 5.26)

Application Question

4-4. A Japanese car manufacturer is considering opening an assembly plant in central United States. Having seen the devastation a tornado can cause, the managers of the manufacturer are particularly concerned about that cause of loss. Their concern is not just about the physical plant but also about the personnel in the plant in the event of a tornado. What risk control measures can a risk management professional recommend to prevent damage to the plant and injury to the people?

Educational Objective 5

Describe the nature of and the pre-loss and post-loss actions appropriate for water causes of loss.

Key Word or Phrase

Hurricane (p. 5.29)

Review Questions

5-1. How is the approach of a tsunami usually signaled? (p. 5.28)

5-2.   Explain how a warning system, such as the Pacific Tsunami
       Warning System, might be effective in controlling property loss
       caused by flooding. (p. 5.28)

5-3.   Identify pre-loss procedures that can prevent property loss
       exposures resulting from flooding. (p. 5.29)

5-4.   Identify pre-loss actions that can be taken to reduce possible
       property damage from a hurricane. (p. 5.31)

5-5.   Identify pre-loss and post-loss actions that may be used to
       reduce possible property damage caused by snowstorms.
       (pp. 5.33–5.35)

Application Question

5-6. An airline reservation center operates twenty-four hours a day
and seven days a week. The center is intentionally located in
a warm climate where the winter weather rarely causes the
temperature to drop below freezing. Despite that precaution, a
severe ice storm has hit the area. What is a key concern regarding the building that houses the center as the ice continues to
accumulate and what, at this point, can be done?

Educational Objective 6

Describe the nature of and the pre-loss and post-loss actions appropriate for land causes of loss.

Key Words and Phrases

Richter Scale (p. 5.38)

Modified Mercalli Intensity Scale (p. 5.38)

Box action design (p. 5.39)

Frame action design (p. 5.39)

Sinkhole (p. 5.42)

Review Questions

6-1.   Identify the factors that contribute to the extent of harm resulting from an earthquake. (p. 5.38)

6-2.   Describe the two measurements used to assess the energy released from an earthquake. (p. 5.38)

6-3.   Explain why location is a key factor in controlling damage caused by earthquakes. (p. 5.39)

6-4.   Identify appropriate pre-loss and post-loss actions that may be used to reduce losses resulting from landslide or mudslide. (p. 5.40)

▶▶

Application Question

6-5.   A restaurant was opened twenty years ago overlooking the scenic view of a valley. This year, several large office buildings were built on either side of the restaurant, also overlooking the valley. Soon after the office buildings were completed, the owner of the restaurant noticed the exterior walls closest to the office buildings had pulled away from the roof. What should the owner do?

Educational Objective 7
Describe the nature of and the pre-loss and post-loss actions appropriate for other property causes of loss.

Key Word or Phrase
Collapse (p. 5.45)

Review Questions

7-1.   Identify possible causes of loss resulting from a thunderstorm. (p. 5.44)

7-2.   Explain how a building collapse may occur. (p. 5.45)

7-3.   Identify the appropriate pre-loss actions for reducing or eliminating potential loss exposures from collapse. (p. 5.46)

7-4.   Identify the post-loss actions for hazardous material losses. (p. 5.47)

Application Question

7-5.   Fast Food Restaurant (Fast Food) has 100 company-owned stores. All of the stores are of an identical design and are built by a single builder. This year, the 5 oldest stores have collapsed. How might Fast Food's risk management professional address this trend with its remaining stores?

Educational Objective 8

Describe the shutdown procedures that are appropriate after a disaster.

Review Questions

8-1. Identify the purpose of an organization's shutdown procedures in a non-disaster-related shutdown. (p. 5.47)

8-2. Describe the shutdown procedure priority in a disaster-related shutdown. (p. 5.47)

8-3. Describe additional disaster recovery plan procedures essential for businesses that consider continuous operations vital to their survival. (p. 5.48)

Application Question

8-4.   Holiday Candy Manufacturer (Holiday) is forced to shut down its facility following the derailment of a railroad car carrying toxic gas. Because this event occurred during Holiday's peak season, Holiday's management is concerned about whether the business can continue to operate even after the toxic gas hazard has been cleared. What steps, if any, should Holiday's risk management professional take regarding its employees to address this concern?

Answers to Assignment 5 Questions

NOTE: These answers are provided to give students a basic understanding of acceptable types of responses. They often are not the only valid answers and are not intended to provide an exhaustive response to the questions.

Educational Objective 1

1-1. The following are the four fundamental concepts of disaster recovery and how a risk management professional effectively applies these concepts:

   (1) Definition of a disaster—a disaster is an event that is so significant it triggers implementation of an organization's disaster recovery plan. By planning in advance, the risk management professional's ability to coordinate the actions of personnel during the disaster can decrease the resulting loss severity.

   (2) Phases of a disaster—a disaster tends to follow a certain pattern or life-cycle. A risk management professional must take many actions in proper sequence to protect essential resources and achieve optimal recovery from a disaster.

   (3) Goals of disaster recovery—include pre-loss and post-loss goals that follow closely the goals of a risk management program. A risk management professional identifies property causes of loss and develops goals to deal with those causes.

   (4) Key considerations for disaster recovery—includes causes of loss, length of warning time, and pre-loss and post-loss actions. Each cause of loss has implications for how a risk management professional can control losses. Similarly, length of warning time affects the availability of disaster recovery options and type of disaster determines which pre-loss and post-loss actions are appropriate.

1-2. The four phases of a disaster are as follows:

   Phase 1: Threat—when the likelihood of a major loss increases rapidly but when the cause of loss has not yet occurred

   Phase 2: Warning—when the occurrence of a cause of loss and a potentially severe loss are imminent

   Phase 3: Impact—when major injury or damage is occurring

   Phase 4: Recovery—when the consequences of damage are dealt with

1-3. The four pre-loss goals of disaster recovery are as follows:

   (1) Economy of operations

   (2) Tolerable uncertainly

   (3) Legality

   (4) Social responsibility

1-4. The six post-loss goals of disaster recovery are as follows:

   (1) Survival

   (2) Continuity of operations

   (3) Profitability

   (4) Earning stability

   (5) Social responsibility

   (6) Growth

1-5.   The three key considerations of disaster recovery are (1) causes of loss of disasters, (2) length of warning time for disasters, and (3) pre-loss and post-loss actions for disasters.

1-6.   The three general categories of causes of loss of disasters are (1) natural causes of loss, (2) the actions of individuals or groups, and (3) general economic conditions.

1-7.   The risk management professional should pay most attention to natural causes of loss and the actions of individuals or groups rather than general economic conditions because the first two categories respond to risk control measures. Losses caused by general economic conditions are typically beyond the control of any one individual or organization.

Educational Objective 2

2-1.   When developing a disaster recovery plan, a risk management professional should take account of purpose, focus, procedures, and key elements.

2-2.   An effective disaster recovery planning process should include the following:
- Adequate time to have an effective plan in place before a cause of loss strikes
- Opportunity to investigate contingency plans for different potential scenarios
- Organization and training of personnel for appropriate disaster recovery responses
- Advance planning of coordinated efforts with public officials and agencies

2-3.   The major areas addressed by effective disaster recovery are as follows:
- Loss prevention
- Loss reduction
- Disaster recovery coordination
- Post-disaster recovery actions

2-4.   The factors used by a catastrophe model to generate projections are as follows:
- Physical characteristics of the loss exposure
- Statistical probability of loss based on past loss trends
- Insurance data

2-5.   An organization might tailor a disaster response to a disaster situation by establishing the following procedures:
- Involve management in disaster recovery plan development and implementation
- Maintain detailed drawings of each facility
- Develop at least two separate and independent evacuation routes for personnel from each building
- Develop procedures to shut down potentially hazardous operations so that they do not exacerbate the disaster and can be protected from further damage
- Develop procedures to report plant emergencies to public agencies
- Maintain a current roster of all employees
- Review the disaster recovery plan with new employees and annually with all others
- Conduct practice drills in cooperation with the public agencies that would normally respond to the organization's emergencies

2-6.   The key elements that should be safeguarded during an emergency to restore normal operations after a disaster are as follows:

- Organizational structure
- Personnel
- Production facilities
- Operating funds
- Market standing

2-7.   A written disaster recovery procedures manual generally includes the following information:

- Structure of the disaster recovery hierarchy, including the chain of command and the composition and general responsibilities of the disaster teams appointed
- Evacuation instructions, including explanations of alarm signals and exit route diagrams
- Loss prevention and loss reduction measures organized by cause of loss, including pre-loss and post-loss actions
- Procedures, addresses, and telephone numbers for contacting the fire, police, medical, and pollution-control services, and other sources of help, including the organization's senior management
- Communication procedures during and after a disaster

2-8.   Individuals on a crisis management team should possess the following characteristics:

- Be physically and psychologically able to fulfill disaster duties
- Be able to function well under stress
- Be available on the premises when the disaster occurs
- Be cross-trained and able to assume the duties of any unavailable team members

2-9.   An organization's disaster recovery plan should implement the given elements for the following reasons:

a.   Production facilities—the organization's value stems from its ability to produce a product or service. A disaster recovery plan should project how a disaster could affect the operation, and develop and test plans to restore or find a temporary substitute for the operation.

b.   Operating funds—the organization must maintain its ability to collect revenues and pay expenses during a disaster. This is accomplished by providing disaster funds and maintaining normal cash inflows and outflows.

c.   Market standing—during a disaster, the organization must preserve its standing in markets in which it sells, buys materials, hires personnel, or obtains funds. A disaster recovery plan needs a prearranged media strategy to keep parties informed.

2-10.   Following a disaster, Pharmaceutical Manufacturer needs to reassure several parties that will be concerned about whether the company will be able to continue to function. Those parties include employees, customers, key suppliers, investors, and the general public. The employees need to be assured that Pharmaceutical Manufacturer will continue to provide them with a place of employment. This assurance is particularly important to key personnel. Customers need to be assured that they can still count on Pharmaceutical Manufacturer for the supply of the drugs they need for their healthcare. Key suppliers need to be assured that Pharmaceutical Manufacturer will continue to order their products and will remain viable and therefore be worthy of the same favorable credit terms. Finally, the general public needs to be assured that Pharmaceutical Manufacturer will remain viable in order to maintain goodwill.

Educational Objective 3

3-1.   An organization should establish a disaster recovery plan to handle temperature extremes causes of loss because the majority of organizations operate most efficiently in a relatively narrow range of temperatures.

3-2.   The focus of a disaster recovery plan created for fire and explosion should focus on pre-loss actions because these causes of loss typically occur with little warning. Pre-loss measures are designed to be automatic and might include the installation of automatic sprinklers, fire-resistive and explosion-dampening walls, and automatic signaling devices for summoning the fire department.

3-3.   The wind chill index is an indication of the cooling effects of wind speed. It is a better indicator than temperature alone because the effects of the lowered temperature indicated by the wind chill index can be more pronounced than the nominal temperature without the wind chill index.

3-4.   Building design features that may be needed in Mexico Distributor's Canadian warehouse that do not exist in its Mexican warehouse include the following:
   • Building insulation adequate for the cold weather climate to reduce heat loss and also provide a barrier against cooler outside air temperatures
   • Properly designed heating systems of adequate size
   • Backup diesel generators to keep furnaces operating during a power outage
   • Buildings positioned to exploit natural terrain features that modify severe weather influences and buildings designed with minimal openings on the prevailing weather side
   • Temporary heating devices to maintain temperatures, shut off exposed systems, and keep protective systems in service
   • Fire protection equipment for subfreezing temperatures

Educational Objective 4

4-1.   Pre-loss actions in a disaster recovery plan for windstorm causes of loss include the following:
   • Design buildings and outside structures to withstand anticipated wind loads
   • Provide storm shutters and blinds for windows and other openings
   • Maintain roof and wall systems and provide adequate supports for outside structures
   • Secure materials and equipment located in areas surrounding the facility

4-2.   Tornadoes exhibit the following characteristics:
   • Generally occur between 3:00 PM and 7:00 PM
   • Move from southwest to northeast
   • Travel about four miles along a front 300–400 yards long
   • Travel at 25–40 mph
   • Have wind velocities of 200–300 mph
   • Last about six to ten minutes

4-3. Predicting the occurrence of tornadoes is difficult because of the following:
- Exact location cannot be pinpointed in advance
- Time of occurrence cannot be pinpointed in advance
- Path of the tornado is erratic

4-4. Central United States covers many states, some of which have a higher propensity for tornadoes than others. Selecting a location with the lowest tornado propensity, while still meeting the other criteria that management has for a location, will help lower the frequency of occurrence. Building the physical plant to withstand the intense tornado winds—for example, by using reinforced concrete—will likely be impractical. Protecting the personnel will also be a challenge. The exact location and time of occurrence of a tornado cannot be pinpointed in advance and it is not always possible to give an advance warning of a tornado. However, constructing underground shelters is a proven measure in saving lives. Therefore, having a shelter in close proximity that plant personnel can quickly enter in the event of a tornado is a sound risk control measure.

Educational Objective 5

5-1. The approach of a tsunami is usually signaled by an unusual fluctuation in coastal water levels.

5-2. A warning system, such as the Pacific Tsunami Warning System, can assist in controlling property loss caused by flooding by providing enough warning time for people to move to higher ground and protect their property.

5-3. Pre-loss procedures that can prevent property loss exposures resulting from flooding include the following:
- Evaluate locations of operations
- Evaluate building sites for flood potential
- Analyze existing structures in flood zones
- Use temporary levees, shutters, and barriers
- Stock disaster supplies
- Place main electrical service equipment on upper floors

5-4. Pre-loss actions that can be taken to reduce possible property damage from a hurricane include the following:
- Design structures to withstand high winds
- Properly maintain building roof supports for outside structures and tie downs for structures of inferior construction
- Move yard stocks inside a substantial structure or protect them against high winds and localized flooding
- Board and tape doors, windows, and other openings
- Maintain disaster power equipment to provide utility services, operate pumps, and maintain protection systems

5-5. Pre-loss actions that may reduce possible property damage caused by snowstorms include the following:
- Design all buildings and structures to withstand at least the anticipated snow loads
- Provide disaster power equipment to backup utility services, operate pumps, and maintain fire protection systems
- Use portable heating devices to keep waterlines from freezing
- Have materials available to make temporary structural bracing and disaster repairs

Post-loss actions that may reduce possible property damage caused by snowstorms include the following:
- Clear roofs of snow accumulation and keep drains, gutters, downspouts, and roof scuppers clean and clear
- Maintain site and building access for disaster, fire, and utility services
- Coordinate all activities with appropriate public officials

5-6. A key concern is collapse of the building as the accumulation of the ice adds more weight on the roof than it was designed to or is maintained to withstand. However, it may be possible to obtain materials for temporary structural bracing and disaster repairs. Disaster equipment may also be obtained to provide utility services and to maintain protection systems. Staff can use portable fuel–fired heaters to meet space heating requirements and to reduce ice accumulations on building surfaces. Also, if personnel have been trained to handle disaster operations, they can provide assistance including placing temporary structural supports, removing ice accumulations, and operating disaster equipment.

Educational Objective 6

6-1. The following factors contribute to the extent of harm resulting from an earthquake:
- The energy released at the earthquake's epicenter (origin)
- The distance between the epicenter and the persons or property exposed to damage
- The ability of exposed persons or property to withstand the earthquake's force

6-2. The two measurements used to assess the energy released from an earthquake are as follows:

(1) Richter Scale—describes the earth's movement in units of magnitude, typically ranging from one to eight, but theoretically unlimited. A one-unit increase represents a thirty-fold increase in energy released at the epicenter.

(2) Modified Mercalli Intensity Scale—a twelve-level set of descriptions of an earthquake's effects at a specified location. An earthquake's given Richter magnitude will have different levels of Modified Mercalli Intensity at different distances from the epicenter.

6-3. Location is a key factor in controlling damage caused by earthquakes for the following reasons:
- People and property located farther away from volcanic areas and major geological faults are less likely to experience detectable earthquakes than those located near such areas.
- People and structures situated on stable earth that can absorb most earthquake shock waves tend to suffer less harm than those located on more unstable ground.

6-4. Pre-loss actions that may be used to reduce losses from landslide or mudslide include the following:
- Conducting a professional survey
- Altering slope or configuration
- Installing natural features to deflect the slide
- Increasing structural supports
- Relocating the structure to a more geographically stable location

Post-loss action that may be used to reduce losses from landslide or mudslide include the following:
- Providing temporary support for stressed building members
- Inspecting any facilities in a landslide area for damage and protecting it from further harm
- Beginning salvage and cleanup
- Coordinating activities with public authorities

6-5. It is possible that the soil supporting the restaurant has been weakened by the office buildings, causing soil deterioration. The owner should confirm this condition by investigating the surface and subsurface conditions thoroughly, taking borings and samples for analysis, and having a qualified geologist or licensed mining engineer perform a detailed study to determine if the soil's ability to support the structure of the restaurant has been compromised. If soil deterioration is confirmed, the structures of the restaurant need to be shored up by using wider footings and/or bracing the structural load on a more stable formation. The owner should also fill deteriorated areas with more stable material, such as concrete and rock.

Educational Objective 7

7-1. Possible causes of loss resulting from a thunderstorm include the following:
- Moderately heavy rainfall
- Lightning
- Tornadoes
- Rainfall sufficient to cause flash flooding
- Hailstorm
- Wind velocity sufficient to uproot trees and damage buildings

7-2. A building collapse may occur from improper design, installation, or structural component maintenance, and from overloading a structure beyond the originally designed capacity. Elements prone to collapse are columns, roof supports, and reinforcing bracing.

7-3. Pre-loss actions for reducing or eliminating potential loss exposures from collapse include the following:
- Maintain adequate clearance between storages and mobile equipment to support members and use barriers around column bases and corners of upright columns
- Treat surfaces of structural elements with rust/corrosion/rot inhibitors
- Adhere to recommended roof and floor loads
- Keep roof drains clear
- Promptly remove accumulations of ice and snow

7-4.   Post-loss actions for hazardous materials losses include using mechanical devices to close off contaminated areas or to trap spills, sounding alarms to evacuate personnel, and implementing procedures for notifying public fire and environmental protection agencies, as well as alerting the organization's disaster crew.

7-5.   Fast Food's risk management professional might investigate the integrity of the remaining stores' structural components, design flaws, and whether the structures are being overloaded, such as by an air conditioning unit.

Educational Objective 8

8-1.   The purpose of an organization's shutdown procedures in a non-disaster-related shutdown is to protect the facilities from damage or deterioration and to be able to resume production with minimal delay.

8-2.   The shutdown procedure priority in a disaster-related shutdown is as follows:

- Follow procedures that, if not taken, would cause greater loss of future ability to operate
- Safeguard property against fire, theft, vandalism, or other causes of loss typical of unoccupied property
- Notify customers and suppliers of the shutdown so that they can find alternative sources or cease their own supply activities

8-3.   Additional disaster recovery plan procedures that are essential for businesses that consider continuous operations vital to their survival include the following:

- An early and ongoing senior management evaluation of the organization's ability to continue operations on its primary premises
- Activating the transfer plans if deemed necessary

8-4.   Holiday should notify its employees of the status of the premises and of their continuing employment status and benefits. To promptly reopen the facilities, personnel must be ready to return to work. Furthermore, some personnel might be required to enter the premises after it has been shut down to inspect production machinery or to verify that fire and burglar alarms remain operational.

Direct Your Learning

Controlling Personnel Loss Exposures

Educational Objectives

After learning the content of this assignment, you should be able to:

1. Describe the human resource potential of an organization and the factors that affect it.

2. Describe the following personnel causes of loss:

    a. Work-related injury and illness

    b. Retirement and resignation

    c. Work-related violence

3. Explain how the following risk control techniques can be used to control the work-related injury and illness cause of loss:

    a. Avoidance

    b. Loss prevention

    c. Loss reduction

    d. Separation and duplication

4. Explain how to control the employee retirement and resignation cause of loss.

5. Explain how to control the work-related violence causes of loss.

6. Define or describe each of the Key Words and Phrases for this assignment.

Study Materials

Required Reading:
- Risk Control
  - Chapter 6

Study Aids:
- SMART Online Practice Exams
- SMART Study Aids
  - Review Notes and Flash Cards— Assignment 6

Outline

▶ **Human Resource Potential**

▶ **Personnel Causes of Loss**

    A. Work-Related Injury and Illness

    B. Retirement and Resignation

    C. Work-Related Violence

▶ **Risk Control for Work-Related Injury and Illness**

    A. Avoidance

    B. Loss Prevention

        1. Safety Engineering

        2. Workplace Design

        3. Workplace Design Programs

    C. Loss Reduction

        1. Potential for Rehabilitation

        2. Rehabilitation Program

    D. Separation and Duplication

▶ **Risk Control for Retirement and Resignation**

▶ **Risk Control for Work-Related Violence**

    A. Workplace Violence

    B. Kidnap and Ransom

▶ **Summary**

▶ **Appendix: Representative Risk Control Measures Against Violent Attack**

Consult the registration booklet that accompanied this course guide for complete information regarding exam dates and fees. Plan to register with the Institutes well in advance of your exam. If you have any questions, or need updated registration information, contact the Institutes (see page iv).

For each assignment, you should define or describe each of the Key Words and Phrases and answer each of the Review and Application Questions.

Educational Objective 1

Describe human resource potential of an organization and the factors that affect it.

Review Questions

1-1.   Identify the possible causes of personnel loss. (p. 6.3)

1-2.   Describe the relationship between an organization's employee productivity and the organization's productivity and value. (p. 6.3)

1-3.   Identify factors that affect the human resource potential of an organization's workforce. (p. 6.4)

Application Question

1-4.   A large percentage of the most productive inside sales representatives for Gamma, a financial services firm, have either
left or are considering leaving to work for a local competi-
tor. Concerned about the loss of valuable personnel, the risk
management professional for the organization investigates
the cause of the resignations. She determines the reason is
not for a substantially higher salary. Instead, the answers she
hears include a safer and less stressful work environment and
promised opportunities for promotion. The most common
response she gets, however, is that the most respected and
productive co-workers have already left. The new firm also has
a reputation of providing scholarships to promising students in
the local community in financial need. Explain which of the
factors listed in the previous question apply to this case.

Educational Objective 2

Describe the following personnel causes of loss:

a.   Work-related injury and illness

b.   Retirement and resignation

c.   Work-related violence

Key Words and Phrases

Ergonomic stress (p. 6.7)

Ionizing radiation (p. 6.7)

Nonionizing radiation (p. 6.7)

Review Questions

2-1.   Identify major loss exposures for personnel causes of loss.
        (p. 6.5)

2-2.   Distinguish between work-related injury and illness. (p. 6.5)

2-3.   Briefly describe the four factors that produce the majority of
        work-related injury causes of loss in manufacturing and retail
        businesses. (p. 6.6)

2-4.   Identify the primary sources of worksite causes of loss likely to
        produce disabling illness. (p. 6.6)

2-5.   What are three modes of entry of chemicals that might result
        in illness causes of loss? (p. 6.7)

2-6. Describe the possible consequences of workplace violence that a risk management professional needs to consider in the risk control plan for an organization. (p. 6.9)

Application Question

2-7. John is employed as a ground crewman at a Canadian airport. He spends most of his workday signaling pilots where to park at a terminal. His job requires him to be outside signaling planes regardless of the noise from the jet engines. Describe two work-site causes of loss that John is exposed to and why they have the potential to produce disabling injuries.

Educational Objective 3

Explain how the following risk control techniques can be used to control the work-related injury and illness cause of loss:

a. Avoidance

b. Loss prevention

c. Loss reduction

d. Separation and duplication

Key Words and Phrases

Ergonomics (p. 6.14)

Manual materials handling (p. 6.14)

Cumulative trauma disorder (CTD) (p. 6.15)

Human factors engineering (p. 6.18)

Biomechanics (p. 6.18)

Review Questions

3-1. Briefly describe two loss prevention measures that an organization might implement to reduce or prevent work-related injuries and illnesses. (pp. 6.11–6.14)

3-2. Identify two basic causes of loss associated with industrial hygiene and the possible safety engineering controls that an organization might implement to limit losses. (pp. 6.11–6.13)

3-3. Explain how workplace design can be implemented by an organization to improve the risk control of loss exposures. (p. 6.14)

3-4.   Identify six major areas of ergonomic concern addressed through workplace design. (p. 6.14)

3-5.   Describe the effects of the following on workplace design:

    a. Occupational Safety and Health Administration (OSHA) (p. 6.14)

    b. 1990 Americans with Disabilities Act (ADA) (p. 6.18)

3-6.   What must an organization do to establish a successful workplace design program? (p. 6.19)

3-7.   Describe the types of rehabilitation that help an organization to control costs of bodily injury claims for employees and other claimants. (p. 6.21)

3-8. Describe the appropriate process for an organization when responding to an injury or disability. (pp. 6.24–6.25)

3-9. Identify circumstances that may limit the effectiveness of a rehabilitation program and that must be managed. (pp. 6.25–6.27)

Application Question

3-10. Jane is the manager of a grocery store. She employs thirty-six people at the store. At any one time, she has six employees not show up for work because of injury or illness. Consequently, she frequently does not have enough cashiers or produce clerks to accommodate peak traffic hours of a day. She has heard about the risk control technique of duplication—specifically, cross-training. What can a risk management consultant tell Jane and her employees to convince them that cross-training is worth the cost and the time to be trained?

Educational Objective 4

Explain how to control the employee retirement and resignation cause of loss.

Review Questions

4-1.   Identify the two purposes of risk control for employee retirement and resignation. (p. 6.28)

4-2.   Describe two ways to identify key managers, officers, owners, and other key personnel in an organization. (p. 6.28)

4-3.   List measures that an organization might use to retain key employees. (p. 6.29)

Application Question

4-4.   A law firm contacted a risk management professional to help it set up a succession plan to use when a senior partner retires. What should the risk management professional tell the managing partner of the law firm?

Educational Objective 5

Explain how to control the work-related violence cause of loss.

Review Questions

5-1. By whom may workplace violence be brought about? (p. 6.29)

5-2. Describe how an organization uses risk control measures to control work-related violence from a co-worker in the following areas: (p. 6.30)

a. Hiring process

b. Supervisor training

c. Written policies

d. Procedural safeguards

e. Termination process

5-3. Identify loss prevention measures an organization might use to protect and secure personnel in high-risk areas. (p. 6.31)

Application Question

5-4. A terrorist cell looking to fund its activities kidnaps for ransom the CFO of an organization. What actions can the organization take at this point to bring the employee home safely?

Answers to Assignment 6 Questions

NOTE: These answers are provided to give students a basic understanding of acceptable types of responses. They often are not the only valid answers and are not intended to provide an exhaustive response to the questions.

Educational Objective 1

1-1. A personnel loss might be caused by the death, disability, retirement, or resignation of an organization's key employee or by reduced productivity caused by work-related violence.

1-2. An organization's productivity depends primarily on the people it employs. The greater the productivity of its employees, the greater the organization's productivity and value.

1-3. Factors that affect the human resource potential of an organization's workforce include the following:
   - Health and education of the general population
   - Proper personnel selection procedures
   - Sound processes for placing, developing, and promoting employees
   - Preservation of employees' existing productive capabilities
   - Rehabilitation of injured or ill employees
   - Retention of productive employees

1-4. The competing firm has demonstrated its support of the local general population's education by providing scholarships. That may positively influence the quality and potential productivity of the firm's future employees. However, that may not be a directly motivating factor for an employee of another firm to come and work there.

   The fact the most respected and productive co-workers have already been hired by the new firm is an indication it is using sound personnel selection, which in turn has encouraged other former co-workers to join the new firm. Providing a safer and less stressful working environment preserves the employees' existing productive capacities. These differences between the firms and the promised opportunities for promotion have had an influence on Gamma's ability to retain its employees.

Educational Objective 2

2-1. Major loss exposures for personnel causes of loss include the following:
   - Work-related injury and illness
   - Retirement and resignation
   - Work-related violence

2-2. Work-related injuries are usually caused by an external physical force exerting stress on the human body resulting in some externally manifested injury. Work-related illness usually develops more slowly as the result of some organic or inorganic agent being absorbed, ingested, inhaled, or injected that impairs a function of the body.

2-3. The four factors that produce the majority of work-related injury causes of loss in manufacturing and retail businesses are as follows:

   (1) Machinery and equipment use—includes production and materials-handling equipment

(2) Materials handling—includes activities associated with moving materials around the workplace, such as raw materials, components, work-in process, and finished goods

(3) Vehicle fleet operations—includes activities related to operation of fleet of cars, trucks, or buses

(4) Physical conditions of premises—includes land and buildings

2-4. The primary sources of worksite causes of loss likely to produce disabling illness are as follows:

- Long-term chemical exposures
- Noise levels
- Ergonomic stress
- Radiation
- Temperature extremes
- Poor air quality

2-5. Three modes of entry of chemicals that might result in illness causes of loss are (1) ingestion, (2) absorption, and (3) inhalation.

2-6. Possible consequences of workplace violence include the death or injury of employees. The risk management professional needs to consider the associated consequences such as lost productivity, cost to replace the employee, workers' compensation claims, life insurance claims, lawsuits, bad publicity, and increases in employee sick days.

2-7. Two worksite causes of loss that John is exposed to are noise levels and temperature extremes. The noise from the jet engines can be excessive, resulting in premature hearing loss. The key determinants of whether the noise exposure is harmful are the sound level; the length of exposure; the sound's frequency distribution; and whether the sound pattern is continuous, intermittent, or a series of impact (pounding) sounds. As the airport is located in Canada, the temperature extremes can be harmful to John because he must be outdoors whenever a plane arrives or departs from the terminal. Straining his body's automatic temperature regulators to adjust for conditions that are persistently too hot or too cold endangers his productivity and health.

Educational Objective 3

3-1. Two loss prevention measures that an organization might implement to reduce or prevent work-related injuries and illnesses are as follows:

(1) Safety engineering—includes physical (engineering) controls and procedural (administrative) controls

(2) Workplace design—an applied science that coordinates the physical features, devices, and working conditions within an environment with the capabilities of the people working in that environment

3-2. Two basic causes of loss associated with industrial hygiene are as follows:

(1) Physical causes of loss—result from incorrect physical conditions. Safety engineering controls include the following:

- Materials substitution
- Isolation
- Wet methods
- Guarding

- Ventilation
- Maintenance
- Housekeeping
- Personal protective equipment (PPE)

(2) Procedural causes of loss—result from improper work procedures. Safety engineering controls include the following:

- Process change
- Education and training
- Standard operating procedures (SOPs)
- Proper supervision
- Medical controls
- Job rotation

3-3. Workplace design can be combined with ergonomics, human factors engineering, or with biomechanics to improve an organization's occupational settings, product designs, and living spaces, which might result in improved risk control of loss exposures.

3-4. Six major areas of ergonomic concern addressed through workplace design are as follows:

(1) Manual materials handling

(2) Cumulative trauma disorders

(3) Physical layout of workstations

(4) Displays and controls

(5) Fatigue

(6) Accommodating disabled employees

3-5. The effects on workplace design are as follows:

a. Occupational Safety and Health Administration (OSHA)—has promoted ergonomics to reduce incidents of musculoskeletal disorders (MSDs) and has produced guidelines in the poultry processing industry, retail grocery stores, and in nursing homes.

b. 1990 Americans with Disabilities Act (ADA)—requires employers to make reasonable accommodations in the workplace so a disabled employee can perform essential job tasks. Accommodations frequently include improving access to the workplace, providing specialized equipment, and providing equipment and procedures for evacuation.

3-6. To establish a successful workplace design program, an organization must do the following:

- Obtain senior management commitment to the workplace design program
- Initiate training for supervisors and employees involved in the program
- Encourage supervisors and employees to participate in the program

3-7. The following types of rehabilitation help an organization to control costs of bodily injury claims for employees and other claimants:

- Physical—restores, as much as possible, motor skills impaired by injury or illness
- Psychological—returns a person, as much as possible, to the healthy mental condition the person enjoyed before becoming disabled
- Vocational—enables a person to return, as much as possible, to their previous work tasks

3-8.   The appropriate process for an organization when responding to an injury or disability is as follows:
- Provide immediate medical attention
- Document the injury
- Encourage assessment of the medical condition by a medically competent professional
- Request information including x-rays, diagnosis, medications prescribed, recommended rest and activity, anticipated return-to-work date, physical activity limitations, and physician's specialty
- Establish the control of the information and the rehabilitation program

3-9.   Circumstances that may limit the effectiveness of a rehabilitation program and that must be managed include the following:
- Extended hospitalization
- Uncoordinated medical treatment
- Extensive medication
- Lack of clear diagnosis
- Lack of clear prognosis
- Round-the-clock nursing care
- Non-goal-oriented physical therapy
- Lack of discharge planning
- Lack of specific date for returning to work

3-10. Duplication helps to offset the adverse financial effects of employee injuries or illnesses. If one employee is disabled, a cross-trained employee with acceptable skills can temporarily replace the disabled employee. Cross training can also reduce the employee's exposure to financial loss from injury or illness. If an employee suffers an injury or illness that prevents the employee from performing a particular task, the diversity of skills developed through cross-training increases the employee's ability to perform other tasks that might not be affected by the disability.

Educational Objective 4

4-1.   The two purposes of risk control for employee retirement and resignation are as follows:
(1) To reduce the severity of a personnel loss
(2) To reduce the frequency of personnel loss

4-2.   Two ways to identify key personnel in an organization are as follows:
(1) Studying organizational charts and the job descriptions that accompany those positions
(2) Examining how each person's efforts contribute to the organization by using flowcharts

4-3.   Measures that an organization might use to retain key employees include the following:
- Financial incentives
- Reimbursement of job-related educational expenses
- Recognition and other non-financial benefits, such as reserved parking

4-4.   The first step of identifying the key person is not an issue in this case—it is the senior partner. Recognizing that the retirement of the senior partner is not preventable in the long run, the focus of the succession plan should be on reducing the severity of the financial consequences when retirement does occur. The plan should determine which other people within the law firm can fill in for the key person, either temporarily or permanently. These individuals should be provided with specialized training ahead of time. Another risk control technique is to spread key functions among a number of different employees so that when the senior partner retires, others can quickly fill in.

Educational Objective 5

5-1. Workplace violence might be brought about by the following:
- Co-workers
- A customer in his or her interaction with an employee
- Someone who has a personal relationship with the employee and has come to the job site
- A complete stranger

5-2. An organization uses risk control measures to control work-related violence from a co-worker in the following ways:
  a. Hiring process—screen potential employees (including their criminal history) and conduct drug tests
  b. Supervisor training—train supervisors in recognizing, avoiding, and reporting potential violence, recognizing an offender profile, and how to apply aggression de-escalation techniques
  c. Written policies—indicate which types of conduct are unacceptable and the consequences of such conduct
  d. Procedural safeguards—establish uniform employment procedures and security measures
  e. Termination process—establish and follow termination procedures

5-3. Loss prevention measures an organization might use to protect and secure personnel in high-risk areas include the following:
- Maintaining a low profile
- Employing bodyguards
- Housing employees in walled or secured compounds
- Using armored vehicles for transport
- Providing bullet-proof vests or body armor for employees to wear
- Training employees to recognize potential kidnap situations
- Varying the employees' routine
- Keeping alert to changes in the political and economic environment

5-4. Law enforcement officials can provide procedures for determining optimum strategies for negotiating with kidnappers and if and when it is appropriate to pay a ransom. If payment is deemed appropriate, arrangements have to be made with the organization's bankers and other sources of funds. The payment can be marked so the funds can be traced and identified.

If the organization has obtained kidnap, ransom, and extortion insurance, the policy can be a source of funds. In addition, the insurer may provide access to experts who can also advise an organization's officials during a kidnapping and who can negotiate with the kidnappers on the company's behalf. Using experts, whether provided by an insurer or hired directly, can prevent communication errors, negative publicity, and a disastrous outcome.

Direct Your Learning

Controlling Liability Loss Exposures

Educational Objectives

After learning the content of this assignment, you should be able to:

1. Describe the following liability causes of loss:

   a. Torts

   b. Statutes

   c. Contracts

2. Describe the consequences of legal liability to an organization.

3. Summarize the major types of liability loss exposures.

4. Identify the risk control points at which risk control techniques are expected to be most effective.

5. Describe the loss prevention measures for tort liability, contractual liability, and statutory liability.

6. Describe the loss reduction measures for tort liability, contractual liability, and statutory liability.

7. Given a case, recommend appropriate risk control measures.

8. Define or describe each of the Key Words and Phrases for this assignment.

Outline

▶ **Liability Causes of Loss**

   A. Torts

      1. Negligence

      2. Intentional Torts

      3. Strict Liability Torts

   B. Contracts

   C. Statutes

▶ **Consequences of Legal Liability**

   A. Monetary Damages

   B. Defense Costs

   C. Indirect Losses

   D. Specific Performance or Injunction

▶ **Liability Loss Exposures**

▶ **Risk Control Techniques**

   A. Risk Control Points

   B. Avoidance

   C. Loss Prevention of Tort Liability

      1. Contractual Removal or Limitation of Tort Liability

      2. Transfer of Liability

      3. Hazard Control

   D. Loss Prevention of Contractual Liability

   E. Loss Prevention of Statutory Liability

   F. Loss Reduction of Tort Liability

      1. Initial Response

      2. Treatment of Claimants

      3. Alternative Dispute Resolution

      4. Litigation

      5. Development of Defenses

      6. Participation in Settlement Negotiation

   G. Loss Reduction of Contractual Liability

   H. Loss Reduction of Statutory Liability

   I. Products Liability Example of Preventing Tort Liability

   J. Professional Liability Example of Preventing Tort Liability

▶ **Summary**

For each assignment, you should define or describe each of the Key Words and Phrases and answer each of the Review and Application Questions.

Educational Objective 1

Describe the following liability causes of loss:

a. Torts

b. Statutes

c. Contracts

Key Words and Phrases

Tort (p. 7.4)

Express contract (p. 7.5)

Implied contract (p. 7.5)

Valid contract (p. 7.5)

Void contract (p. 7.5)

Voidable contract (p. 7.6)

Unenforceable contract (p. 7.6)

Review Questions

1-1. Identify the causes of loss from which a liability loss might arise. (p. 7.3)

1-2. Identify the agents through whom an organization may become liable under tort. (p. 7.4)

1-3. Describe three categories of wrongful acts that are classed as torts. (pp. 7.4–7.5)

1-4. Describe the basic requirements for a contract to be enforceable. (p. 7.5)

Application Question

1-5. Hadley Kitchen Fire Suppression Systems (Hadley) sells and services commercial kitchen fire suppression systems. Hadley installs one of its systems into a restaurant. The restaurant owner never signs or returns the Hadley service agreement. Consequently, Hadley never services the system. Following a fire, the restaurant owner sues Hadley for breach of contract. What might Hadley assert in its defense?

Educational Objective 2
Describe the consequences of legal liability to an organization.

Review Questions

2-1. Briefly describe the consequences of incurring legal liability. (pp. 7.6–7.8)

2-2. Distinguish between the following types of compensatory damages: (pp. 7.6–7.7)

a. Special damages

b. General damages

2-3. Describe punitive damages and their purpose. (p. 7.7)

Application Question

2-4. Fernley Crop Dusting Company (Fernley) is sued by homeowners for polluting their property as a consequence of
Fernley's crop dusting operations. As part of the judgment
against Fernley, homeowners are awarded reimbursement
for medical expenses incurred, payment for anxiety Fernley
caused, and a directive that Fernley not over-spray crops
again. Identify the monetary damages Fernley has been
ordered to pay.

Educational Objective 3

Summarize the major types of liability loss exposures.

Key Word or Phrase

Attractive nuisance (p. 7.9)

Review Questions

3-1. Describe premises liability loss exposure and describe the duty of care required for the following individuals: (p. 7.8)

   a. Trespassers

   b. Licensees

3-2. Describe how a liability loss might arise from the following loss exposures: (p. 7.9)

   a. Operations liability loss exposure

   b. Products liability loss exposure

   c. Completed operations liability loss exposure

▶▶

3-3.   Explain how an automobile liability loss might arise other than in relation to operation of a vehicle. (p. 7.9)

Application Question

3-4.   Pizza Delivery delivers 20,000 pizzas per week from ten locations. Identify the liability loss exposures that Pizza Delivery may have.

Educational Objective 4

Identify the risk control points at which risk control techniques are expected to be most effective.

Key Word or Phrase

Risk control point (p. 7.11)

Review Questions

4-1.   Identify risk control points that a risk management professional must evaluate when determining the application of a risk control technique to a liability cause of loss. (p. 7.11)

4-2. Explain why a legal claim must be brought by the harmed party in a breach of contract lawsuit. (p. 7.11)

4-3. Explain why the risk control points apply in allegations of statute violation. (p. 7.11)

Application Question

4-4. Barnton Flooring Installer (Barnton) installs flooring with weak glue. Consequently, some people are injured when the floors shift. This weak glue has been used by Barnton for the last two years. Identify the risk control point that Barnton's risk management professional could address so that its liability loss exposures are minimized.

Educational Objective 5

Describe the loss prevention measures for tort liability, contractual liability, and statutory liability.

Key Words and Phrases

Waiver (p. 7.12)

Hold-harmless agreement (p. 7.13)

Exculpatory agreement, or exculpatory clause (p. 7.13)

Vicarious liability (p. 7.14)

Review Questions

5-1.   Identify loss prevention measures that might be used by an organization as a means of preventing loss by shifting or limiting the duty owed to the party that is harmed. (p. 7.12)

5-2.   Describe clauses that an organization might add to contracts to remove or limit liability. (pp. 7.12–7.13)

5-3.   Explain how an organization might use transfer of liability for
       risk control and risk financing purposes. (p. 7.14)

5-4.   Identify types of contractual agreements that might subject an
       organization to legal responsibilities. (p. 7.18)

5-5.   Identify loss prevention measures an organization might use for
       contractual liability. (p. 7.18)

5-6.   Identify sources an organization might use to gain information
       regarding statutory compliance requirements that might help
       prevent statutory liability losses. (p. 7.18)

5-7.   Describe the process an organization might use in preventing
       statutory liability losses. (p. 7.18)

Application Question

5-8. Alderton Trampoline Manufacturing Company (Alderton) makes trampolines for residential use. What risk control measures might Alderton use for its products?

Educational Objective 6

Describe the loss reduction measures for tort liability, contractual liability, and statutory liability.

Key Words and Phrases

Mediation (p. 7.23)

Arbitration (p. 7.24)

Compulsory arbitration (p. 7.24)

Legal privilege (p. 7.27)

Immunity (p. 7.27)

Assumption-of-risk defense (p. 7.28)

Review Questions

6-1.   List five widely used techniques of alternative dispute resolution (ADR). (p. 7.22)

6-2.   Identify the steps in the litigation process. (p. 7.25)

6-3.   Describe loss reduction measures that an organization might use to reduce the severity of loss from contractual liability. (pp. 7.29–7.30)

6-4.   Explain why most organizations focus attention on loss prevention rather than loss reduction. (p. 7.31)

Application Question

6-5. Waxton Road Building Contractor (Waxton) wants a bonus
      that rewards rapid completion included in its contract with the
      highway department. In addition to the bonus provision, how
      might the highway department further encourage Waxton to
      be on time?

Educational Objective 7

Given a case, recommend appropriate risk control measures.

Application Question

7-1. Rocky Mountain Boot Company (Rocky Mountain) is consid-
      ering which risk control measures to use to prevent a products
      liability exposure. What are some of the measures Rocky
      Mountain might consider?

Answers to Assignment 7 Questions

NOTE: These answers are provided to give students a basic understanding of acceptable types of responses. They often are not the only valid answers and are not intended to provide an exhaustive response to the questions.

Educational Objective 1

1-1. The causes of loss from which a liability loss might arise are tort, contracts, or statutes.

1-2. An organization's tort liability can arise from the following agents:
- Employees
- Subordinates
- Associates
- Directors and officers
- Anyone using the organization's property with its permission
- In some situations, volunteers acting on the organization's behalf

1-3. Three categories of wrongful acts that are classed as torts are as follows:
  (1) Negligence—the tortfeasor exposed others to unreasonable danger by failing to exercise the duty of care the law requires under the circumstances.
  (2) Intentional torts—acts or omissions that the tortfeasor intended, although the consequences may not be intended.
  (3) Strict liability torts—the organization engages in certain activities that are considered hazardous or that involve products liability.

1-4. The basic requirements for a contract to be enforceable are as follows:
- Agreement—one party makes an offer that the other party accepts.
- Consideration—each party gives up something of value.
- Capacity to contract—the parties must have the legal ability to enter into contracts.
- Legal purpose—the contract must have a legal purpose and not be opposed to public policy.

1-5. Hadley might assert in its defense that one or more of the basic requirements of a contract were not met. Hadley did make an offer to the restaurant owner, but the offer was never accepted by the restaurant owner. This basic requirement is a prerequisite to the other elements needed to create an enforceable contract. Without a contract, Hadley would assert that it was under no obligation to service the system and is not liable for damage caused by the fire.

Educational Objective 2

2-1. The consequences of incurring legal liability are as follows:
- Monetary damages—cost of money required to pay for verdicts, settlements, or fines.
- Defense costs—costs for investigation and to prepare a defense when an organization faces a civil suit or criminal charge.
- Indirect losses—includes costs incurred to regain customers because of the filing of a claim against an organization, such as increased advertising expense or a public relations campaign.

- Specific performance or injunction—performance is required as specified in the contract (specific performance) or the firm refrains from doing a particular activity (injunction).

2-2. The types of compensatory damages can be distinguished as follows:

   a. Special damages—specific known loss amounts, such as cost of medical care, repairing damaged property, and restoring lost income

   b. General damages—nonspecific uncertain loss amounts, such as pain and suffering and loss of companionship

2-3. Punitive damages are awarded by a court in excess of the amount necessary to indemnify a party for a loss. The purpose of punitive damages is to modify the wrongdoer's behavior and set an example to avoid reoccurrence of the action.

2-4. Fernley's reimbursement of medical expenses are special damages, while Fernley's payment for the homeowners' anxiety is general damages. Both of these types of damages are monetary damages. The restriction on Fernley's operations is an injunction, and is not considered to be monetary damages.

Educational Objective 3

3-1. Premises liability loss exposure exists when an organization is legally responsible for maintaining safe premises for any visitors to the premises. The following duty of care is required for the specified individuals:

   a. Trespassers—the organization must not make the premises unsafe and must not set traps with the intent of harming a trespasser.

   b. Licensees—the organization must keep the premises safe and must warn licensees of any dangerous conditions.

3-2. A liability loss might arise from the following loss exposures as described:

   a. Operations liability loss exposure—might arise for any organization that conducts operations on their own premises, particularly if the operations create waste products

   b. Products liability loss exposure—might arise if a party claims the organization's product is defective, is faultily designed, or if instructions failed to warn of potential harmful effects

   c. Completed operations liability loss exposure—might arise if bodily injury or property damage is caused by an organization's completed work, including defective parts or materials furnished with the work

3-3. An automobile liability loss might arise other than in relation to operation of a vehicle because a driver of a motor vehicle has a duty to exercise care with the vehicle's maintenance. For example, a driver who knowingly operates a vehicle with faulty brakes, lights, or tires is liable to a passenger who may be injured in an accident related to such a defect.

3-4. Pizza Delivery has at least the following liability loss exposures:

- Premises liability arising from those customers that order pizza at one of Pizza Delivery's ten locations

- Products liability arising from sickness caused by tainted pizza

- Automobile liability arising from the use of vehicles by Pizza Delivery's drivers

- Workers' compensation liability arising from Pizza Delivery's employees

Educational Objective 4

4-1.   Risk control points that a risk management professional must evaluate when determining the application of a risk control technique to a liability cause of loss include the following:
- A duty to act (or not to act) exists.
- A breach of that duty occurs.
- Harm to some other party as a direct result of that breach of duty occurs.
- Proximate cause between the breach and the harm is established.
- The amount of harm that the breach caused is determined.
- A legal claim by the harmed party is submitted.

4-2.   A legal claim must be brought by the harmed party in a breach of contract lawsuit because without a claim being asserted by the harmed party, that party cannot legally force the offending party to honor its promise.

4-3.   The risk control points apply in allegations of statute violation because a statute unilaterally imposes a duty to act or not act.

4-4.   Barnton's risk management professional may be able to minimize liability by contacting customers whose flooring work involved the weak glue. Barnton could then offer to reinstall the flooring with a stronger glue before an injury occurs. The risk control point in this instance is preventing the harm that could occur to some other party as a direct result of a breach of the duty to use a strong enough glue to prevent the floor from shifting.

Educational Objective 5

5-1.   Loss prevention measures that might be used by an organization to prevent loss by shifting or limiting the duty owed to the party that is harmed include the following:
- Contractual removal or limitation of tort liability
- Transfer of liability
- Hazard control

5-2.   Clauses that an organization might add to contracts to remove or limit liability include the following:
- Waivers—voluntary relinquishment of a known right
- Hold-harmless agreements—contractual provisions by which one party (indemnitor) agrees to assume the liability of a second party (indemnitee)
- Exculpatory agreements—contractual provisions that enable a party to avoid liability for negligence or a wrongful act
- Unilateral notices—notices that can limit liability if they are physically apparent, expressed in clear terms, in language the other party understands, and reasonable in extent

5-3.   An organization might transfer liability by subcontracting specific activities to another organization. Transfer serves as a risk control technique when the transfer does not include a duty to indemnify. When transfer does include a duty to indemnify, it is an example of a risk financing technique.

5-4. Types of contractual agreements that might subject an organization to legal responsibilities include leases, purchase orders, sales contracts, shipping agreements, exculpatory agreements, and hold-harmless agreements.

5-5. Loss prevention measures an organization might use for contractual liability include the following:
- To have any contract reviewed by counsel, preferably before it is signed
- To use written contracts rather than oral contracts that accurately reflect both parties' intentions

5-6. Sources an organization might use to gain information regarding statutory compliance requirements are internal experts, external consultants, trade associations, and legal libraries.

5-7. An organization might use the following process to prevent statutory liability losses:
- Understanding statutory compliance requirements applicable to their organization
- Determining how to fulfill the statutory obligations
- Assigning responsibility for statutory compliance
- Monitoring the activities to assure the organization stays in compliance

5-8. Alderton should consider the following risk control measures in manufacturing its products:
- Design the trampoline with safety in mind and consider the potential customers (users) of the product (in this instance children)
- Adhere to established production and quality controls
- Conduct product reliability analysis
- Test its trampolines and packaging before, during, and after development
- Be clear and accurate in any instructions for use
- Have legal counsel review all warning labels, advertising, sale warranties, products use description and instructions, warranties, and dealer instructions
- Implement product servicing and effective complaint-handling procedures
- Conduct product usage analysis

Educational Objective 6

6-1. Five widely used techniques of alternative dispute resolution are as follows:
(1) Voluntary restoration
(2) Negotiation
(3) Mediation
(4) Mini-trial
(5) Arbitration

6-2. The steps in the litigation process are as follows:
- Completing discovery
- Working with legal counsel
- Selecting the jurisdiction

6-3.   Loss reduction measures that an organization might use to reduce the severity of loss from contractual liability include the following:

- Select a favorable jurisdiction—usually a clause is negotiated into the contract that specifies which state's law will govern the contract's interpretation.
- Include limits of liability—attempts to cap the damages payable by one party.
- Include a liquidated damages provision—limits the amount for which one party might otherwise be liable.
- Include a valuation clause—specifies the valuation of property in the event it is lost, stolen, or damaged.
- Evaluate duty to mitigate—the party that claims the other breached the contract has a duty to use good faith efforts to reduce the severity of its losses.

6-4.   Most organizations focus attention on loss prevention rather than loss reduction because few defenses are available to an organization to reduce fine or penalty when a statute is violated.

6-5.   To encourage Waxton's on-time completion, the highway department may consider including a liquidated damages provision in the contract. Such a provision would penalize Waxton in the event of delayed completion.

Educational Objective 7

7-1.   To be thorough, the assessment of risk control measures should be both pre-sale and post-sale. Pre-sale, Rocky Mountain should assess the quality of materials they receive from their suppliers, and the quality and safety of their own manufacturing process. They should also assess the design quality of their boots and the adequacy of their safety testing. Post-sale, Rocky Mountain should assess their complaints handling procedures. Good record keeping is essential both for complaints handling and for any product recalls that might become necessary.

Direct Your Learning

Understanding Claim Administration

Educational Objectives

After learning the content of this assignment, you should be able to:

1. Describe claim administration characteristics.

2. Describe the goals of claim administration.

3. Describe the steps of the claim adjusting process.

4. Explain how to manage the personnel involved and the claim monitoring aspects of claim administration management.

5. Explain how to reduce claim costs using litigation management, advance payments, subrogation, and cost containment of medical claims.

6. Describe the following about loss reserving:

   • Why loss reserving accuracy is important

   • What factors make loss reserving difficult

   • What methods are used to establish loss reserves

   • How to estimate incurred but not reported and allocated loss adjustment expense reserves

7. Define or describe each of the Key Words and Phrases for this assignment.

Study Materials

Required Reading:
▶ Risk Control
  • Chapter 8

Study Aids:
▶ SMART Online Practice Exams
▶ SMART Study Aids
  • Review Notes and Flash Cards— Assignment 8

Outline

▶ **Claim Administration Characteristics**

▶ **Claim Administration Goals**

   A. Enforcing Contractual Obligations

   B. Gathering Claim Data

   C. Reducing the Frequency and Severity of Claims

   D. Estimating the Amount of Claims

   E. Promoting Equitable Compensation

▶ **Claim Adjusting Process**

   A. Acknowledging Loss Notice and Assigning Loss to Claim Representative

   B. Verifying Coverage

   C. Making Initial Contact

   D. Investigating the Claim

   E. Determining the Cause of Loss and Amount of Damages

     1. Reservation of Rights, Nonwaiver Agreements, and Denial Letters

     2. Amount of Damages if Suit Is Filed

     3. Techniques to Determine the Amount of Damages

     4. Cause of Loss and Amount of Property Damage

     5. Cause of Loss and Amount of Bodily Injury Damage

   F. Concluding the Loss

     1. Negotiation

     2. Mediation

     3. Arbitration

     4. General Release

     5. Joint Tortfeasor Release

     6. Release of Minor's Claim

     7. Open-End Release

     8. No-Release Settlement

     9. Structured Settlements

    10. Payment

▶ **Claim Administration Management**

   A. Personnel Involved

     1. Internal Staff

     2. Insurance Claim Representatives

     3. Insurance Agents and Brokers

     4. Third-Party Administrators

   B. Claim Monitoring

     1. Claim Information System

     2. Claim Audits

▶ **Claim Cost Reduction**

   A. Litigation Management

     1. Legal Counsel

     2. Legal Bill Audits

     3. Alternative Fee Arrangements

     4. Defense Plans and Budgets

     5. Status Reports

   B. Advance Payments

   C. Subrogation

     1. Subrogation Principles and Purposes

     2. Subrogation Recovery Apportionment

   D. Cost Containment of Medical Claims

     1. Fee Audits

     2. Utilization Review

▶ **Loss Reserving**

   A. Loss Reserving Accuracy

   B. Loss Reserving Difficulty

     1. Loss Reserving Methods

     2. Incurred but Not Reported (IBNR) Reserve

     3. Allocated Loss Adjustment Expense (ALAE) Reserve

▶ **Summary**

▶ **Appendix A: Questions to Ask of Third-Party Administrator Applicants**

▶ **Appendix B: Suggestions on How to Select an Attorney**

▶ **Appendix C: Sample Billing Guidelines for Attorneys**

▶ **Appendix D: Defense Attorney's Suit Status Report**

▶ **Appendix E: Case Study—How to Use Utilization Review (UR) to Manage Workers' Compensation Claims**

For each assignment, you should define or describe each of the Key Words and Phrases and answer each of the Review and Application Questions.

Educational Objective 1

Describe claim administration characteristics.

Key Words and Phrases

Claim administration (p. 8.3)

Loss adjustment expense (p. 8.4)

Claimant, or payee (p. 8.4)

Claim representative (p. 8.6)

Review Questions

1-1. Identify types of claims that are administered through an organization's claim administration process. (pp. 8.3–8.4)

1-2. Distinguish between first-party claims and third-party claims. (p. 8.4)

1-3.   List the individuals who might be involved in an organization's claim administration. (p. 8.6)

Application Question

1-4.   Acme Delivery Service pays the first $50,000 of each auto claim out of its own funds. One of Acme's drivers went through a red light at an intersection. The claimant's vehicle hit the Acme vehicle on its rear quarter panel. Because the point of impact was at the rear of his vehicle instead of the front or middle, the Acme driver argues that the claimant failed to keep a proper lookout and is at least partially at fault. As Acme can expect to pay something to the claimant, how will questionable liability and having to pay the claim from its own funds likely influence the amount and timing of the payment to the claimant?

Educational Objective 2

Describe the goals of claim administration.

Key Word or Phrase

Ultimate value of a claim (p. 8.7)

Review Questions

2-1.   Identify the goals of claim administration. (p. 8.6)

2-2.   Identify the questions whose answers enable an organization to enforce any applicable contractual obligations for the following types of claim: (p. 8.7)

   a. First-party claim

   b. Third-party claim

2-3.   Explain how gathering claim data regarding events that lead to claims is useful to an organization. (p. 8.7)

2-4.   Describe how an organization might use claim administration to reduce the following (pp. 8.7–8.8)

   a. Frequency of claims

b. Severity of claims

Application Question

2-5. Decades after it started selling its product, a manufacturer
of an insulating material discovers that the product causes a
debilitating lung disease if a person breathes in the product's
fibers. Based on its sales records, the manufacturer knows that
claimants from all over the country could be demanding payments from it over the next several decades as they become
ill. However, it does not know who the claimants could be
or when they will become ill. Nor does it know how much
will be needed to close each of their claims. Explain whether
the ultimate value of claims takes into account these types of
uncertainties.

Educational Objective 3

Describe the steps of the claim adjusting process.

Key Words and Phrases

Closure (p. 8.19)

Settlement (p. 8.19)

Release (p. 8.19)

General release (p. 8.20)

Joint tortfeasors (p. 8.21)

No-release settlement (p. 8.25)

Annuity (p. 8.27)

Contingent liability (p. 8.28)

Review Questions

3-1.   List the six steps in the claim adjusting process. (p. 8.9)

3-2.   List key questions that help a claim representative verify insurance coverage regarding a claim. (p. 8.10)

3-3. Identify the purpose of claim investigation and the informa-
      tion a claim representative gathers when investigating a claim.
      (p. 8.11)

3-4. Describe the following methods used by a claim representative
      to determine the amount of damages of a claim: (p. 8.14)

      a. Individual case method

      b. Roundtable method

      c. Formula method

      d. Expert system method

3-5. Regarding a bodily injury claim, describe the following: (p. 8.15)

    a. Two categories of bodily injury claims

    b. The determinations that are necessary for a claim representative to make with the two categories of bodily injury claims described in (a).

3-6. Describe how a claim representative might determine values for special damages and general damages. (pp. 8.15–8.16)

3-7. Describe the four steps essential in any negotiation to conclude a loss. (pp. 8.18–8.19)

3-8. Describe the following types of releases that might be used once a loss has been successfully negotiated, mediated, or arbitrated:

    a. General release (p. 8.20)

b. Joint tortfeasor release (p. 8.21)

c. Release of minor's claim (p. 8.23)

d. Open-end release (p. 8.25)

3-9.   Describe the types of claimants for whom a structured settle-
       ment is appropriate. (p. 8.28)

Application Question

3-10. Larry is a claim representative with thirty years of experience adjusting auto liability claims. During that time he has reviewed thousands of medical records from claimants alleging injuries from auto accidents. Despite his extensive experience reviewing medical records, explain why Larry would still find obtaining an opinion from an independent medical expert useful.

Educational Objective 4

Explain how to manage the personnel involved and the claim monitoring aspects of claim administration management.

Key Words and Phrases

Staff claim representative (p. 8.30)

Field claim representative (p. 8.30)

Office claim representative (p. 8.30)

Independent adjuster (p. 8.30)

Public adjuster (p. 8.30)

Claim experience report (p. 8.33)

Claim audit (p. 8.35)

Review Questions

4-1. Briefly describe the personnel involved in claim administration management. (pp. 8.29–8.31)

4-2. Identify information that should be included in a contract between a third party administrator (TPA) and the client organization. (p. 8.32)

4-3. Describe the information that should be included in an organization's claim experience reports. (pp. 8.33–8.34)

4-4. Describe the warning signs of difficulty that might arise from a claim audit. (p. 8.35)

▶▶

Application Question

4-5. Jessie is a risk management professional working for Mega Corporation. As part of Mega's corporate governance efforts, its management would like an audit of the corporation's in-house adjusting department to be performed. Who should Jessie hire to perform the audit and what should he expect in the auditor's proposal?

Educational Objective 5

Explain how to reduce claim costs using litigation management, advance payments, subrogation, and cost containment of medical claims.

Key Words and Phrases

Advance payment (p. 8.40)

Subrogation (p. 8.41)

Contractual subrogation (p. 8.42)

Equitable subrogation (p. 8.42)

Fee audit (p. 8.43)

Usual, customary, and reasonable charge (UCR) (p. 8.43)

Utilization review (UR) (p. 8.44)

Review Questions

5-1.   List four ways an organization can reduce the costs of restoring its first-party and third-party claims. (p. 8.36)

5-2.   Briefly describe what an organization should consider regarding litigation management. (pp. 8.37–8.40)

5-3.   Identify the principles of subrogation. (p. 8.42)

5-4.   Identify the purposes of subrogation. (p. 8.42)

5-5. Describe two methods an organization might use to contain costs of medical claims. (pp. 8.42–8.44)

Application Question

5-6. Janice is a claim representative for an insurer and is trying to decide whether to offer an advance payment to a claimant who broke her hip when she tripped and fell on a piece of worn carpet in an insured's poorly lit movie theater. The claimant is a retired schoolteacher living on a small pension and without medical insurance. She has been cooperative to date—allowing Janice to record the statement she gave her over the phone. Explain what fact issues Janice should consider when deciding whether to make such an offer.

Educational Objective 6

Describe the following about loss reserving:

- Why loss reserving accuracy is important

- What factors make loss reserving difficult

- What methods are used to establish loss reserves

- How to estimate incurred but not reported and allocated loss adjustment expense reserves

---

Key Words and Phrases

Loss reserves (p. 8.44)

Underreserving (p. 8.45)

Stair-step reserving (p. 8.45)

Overreserving (p. 8.45)

Roundtable technique (p. 8.47)

Average value method (p. 8.47)

Formula method (p. 8.47)

Loss ratio method (p. 8.47)

Review Questions

6-1.   Explain what loss reserves are and the effects of the following:
        (pp. 8.45–8.46)

        a. Underreserving

        b. Overreserving

6-2. Identify the factors that make accurate claim reserving difficult.
       (p. 8.46)

6-3. Explain the situations in which an organization might use the
       following methods of loss reserving: (p. 8.47)

       a. Roundtable technique

       b. Average value method

       c. Formula method

       d. Loss ratio method

**Actively capture information by using the open space in the SMART Review Notes to
write out key concepts. Putting information into your own words is an effective way to
push that information into your memory.**

Application Question

6-4.   Holly is a risk management professional employed by a large
grocery store chain. The chain has recently hired a new chief
financial officer (CFO) who is unfamiliar with what must be
paid in order to close open claims. What should Holly tell her
new CFO to expect?

Answers to Assignment 8 Questions

NOTE: These answers are provided to give students a basic understanding of acceptable types of responses. They often are not the only valid answers and are not intended to provide an exhaustive response to the questions.

Educational Objective 1

1-1.   Types of claims that are administered through an organization's claim administration process include the following:

- Claims made by others against an organization
- Claims an organization makes against an insurer, contractual transferee, or wrongdoer who is legally liable to the organization for its losses
- Claims the organization makes on its own resources for its own losses or for the losses of others to whom it is legally liable

1-2.   First-party claims involve the organization's own property, personnel, or net income losses. Third-party claims involve losses allegedly suffered by another party that the third party claims are the responsibility of the organization.

1-3.   Individuals who might be involved in an organization's claim administration include the following:

- The organization's risk management or legal personnel
- Claim personnel of the organization's insurers
- Third-party administrators (TPAs)

1-4.   In principle, the amount and timing of claim payments should not be affected by the organization's perspective on that claim (payor or payee of funds). In practice, the amount and timing are negotiable. The claimant may believe that his or her claim is worth more and ought to be paid sooner than Acme does. Acme may believe that this claim is unjustified and merits less or no payment. Because an earlier payment is worth more than a later payment, the claimant may want a payment sooner than Acme wants to make a payment.

Educational Objective 2

2-1.   The goals of claim administration are as follows:

- Enforcing contractual obligations
- Gathering claim data
- Reducing the frequency and severity of claims
- Estimating the amount of claims
- Promoting equitable compensation

2-2.   The questions that enable an organization to enforce any applicable contractual obligations are as follows for each type of claim:

a.   First-party claim

- Is any part of the claim covered by a contract?
- What is the extent of the loss?

b. Third-party claim
- Is the organization legally liable for, or morally obligated to pay, the damage sustained by the third party?
- If so, is the claim or any part of it covered by a contract?
- What is the extent of the harm for which the organization is legally or morally obligated?

2-3. Gathering claim data regarding events that lead to claims is useful to an organization because it might do the following:
- Enable the organization to forecast the ultimate value of claims
- Enable the organization to determine how similar events might be prevented
- Reveal loss exposures that might otherwise go undetected or be underestimated
- Provide information on reporting, developing, and closing claims that is useful in forecasting claim development
- Provide information useful in determining trend factors
- Document the effectiveness of risk control efforts

2-4. An organization's claim administration efforts can reduce frequency and severity of claims in the following ways:
a. Frequency of claims—by carefully determining whether liability exists and then rejecting fraudulent or groundless claims
b. Severity of claims—by monitoring the extent of damages including requiring claimants to substantiate their damages, by documenting and analyzing the circumstances of losses, and by claiming losses under insurance policies or risk transfer contracts

2-5. The ultimate value of a claim is the dollar amount of the claim payment plus the claim adjustment expenses. In this situation, the potential claimants are widely dispersed geographically, high in number, likely not homogeneous, and will assert their claims over an extended period of time— possibly several decades. The ultimate value of a claim can take these variables into account but, because of these wide ranging variables, the value will only be a rough estimate until the losses are actually closed.

Educational Objective 3

3-1. The six steps in the claim adjusting process are as follows:
(1) Acknowledging loss notice and assigning loss to a claim representative
(2) Verifying coverage
(3) Making initial contact
(4) Investigating the claim
(5) Determining the cause of the loss and amount of damages
(6) Concluding the loss

3-2. Key questions that help a claim representative verify insurance coverage regarding a claim include the following:
- Does the loss fall within the policy's effective dates?
- Who is the insured in the policy?

- What is insured by the policy?
- What causes of loss are covered by the policy?
- Do any exclusions apply to the loss?
- Is the amount of recovery limited by the policy?

3-3. The purpose of claim investigation is to gather evidence to enable the evaluation, settlement, or resistance of the claim. Information a claim representative gathers in the process of investigation includes the following:

- Accident or other event causing the damage or injury
- Resulting damage or injury
- Possible legal liability of any party for having caused that damage or injury
- Potential sources of recovery for payments owed to or collectible from others

3-4. The following methods are used by a claim representative to determine amounts of damages of a claim:

a. Individual case method—uses a value based on the totality of a claim's circumstances and the claim representative's experience in similar cases

b. Roundtable method—uses a value determined though claim evaluation by two or more claim representatives who determine a consensus figure or take the average of the amounts suggested

c. Formula method—uses a value determined by a mathematical formula based on the assumption that a ratio exists between medical costs and general damages awarded

d. Expert system method—uses a value determined by a computer program designed to identify and simulate the thought processes of experienced, knowledgeable claim representatives

3-5. a. Two categories of bodily injury claims are workers' compensation and injuries to third parties.

b. For workers' compensation claims, the claim representative determines whether the injury is covered under the applicable workers' compensation statute and if covered, determines the amount and types of benefits to be paid. For injuries to third parties, the claim representative determines if legal liability exists and if liability exists, obtains information about special and general damages.

3-6. A claim representative might determine values for special damages by verifying amounts of damages claimed, what damages are reasonable and necessary, and whether the damages are related to the accident. General damages are subjective and based on testimony of medical providers; the injured party; and others, such as employers, family members, and friends who are aware of the severity, intensity, and duration of the suffering.

3-7. The four steps essential in any negotiation to conclude a loss are as follows:

(1) Preparation—gathering information to enable the negotiator to develop strategies to resolve the dispute effectively and amicably.

(2) Exploration—opening discussions allow exploration of each party's positions, perceptions, and concerns to allow for meaningful negotiations and possible agreement.

(3) Exchanges of offers and counteroffers—a summary of agreed upon facts, areas of dispute, and unresolved issues provides a foundation for reasonable offers and equitable alternatives. When parties cannot resolve their differences, alternatives include litigation, mediation, and arbitration.

(4) Closure and settlement—parties have resolved their differences and, in many cases, have also signed a formal written agreement.

3-8.   The following types of releases might be used once a loss has been successfully negotiated, mediated, or arbitrated:

a.   General release—frees the first-party indemnitor in a third-party claim from all further claims arising out of the loss for which a specific sum is paid as legal consideration

b.   Joint tortfeasor release—releases joint tortfeasors but preserve a claimant's rights against other wrongdoers not explicitly released

c.   Release of minors' claim—executed by the parents, the surviving parent, or guardian of a third-party claimant who is a minor

d.   Open-end release—used when the extent of harm suffered by the claimant is known and most of the needed restoration has been provided, but some additional small payments might be required in the future

3-9.   The types of claimants for whom a structured settlement is appropriate include the following:

- Individuals who have difficulty managing money
- Minors whose settlements frequently require court approval
- Persons who are seriously injured or disabled
- Dependents with death claims

3-10. Despite his extensive experience, Larry does not have the specialized training, education, experience, and technology to determine the extent of disability and needed course of treatment. Therefore, obtaining a qualified medical opinion would still be useful.

Educational Objective 4

4-1.   The personnel involved in claim administration management are as follows:

- Internal staff—protect the organization's indemnification rights and fulfill its indemnitor obligations. Includes staff in the risk management department, departmental managers, and others involved in claims.
- Insurance claim representatives—often negotiate payment for a loss with the organization's insurer. Staff claim representatives and independent adjusters always represent insurers; public adjusters usually represent insured organizations.
- Insurance agents and brokers—usually operate according to detailed instructions and limitations about the types and amounts of claims they can settle. Their authority is often limited to small uncomplicated losses.
- Third-party administrators—negotiate claims or perform other duties regarding retained, insured, or otherwise transferred losses.

4-2.   Information that should be included in a contract between a TPA and the client organization includes the following:

- Scope of the TPA's authority regarding a settlement
- Details of the services the TPA is to provide to the client organization
- Procedures by which the TPA will notify the client organization, its insurers, and legal counsel about claims that are unusual

▶▶

- Ownership and access rights to the client organization's and the TPA's working files
- Minimum amounts and types of fidelity and surety bonds and professional liability insurance that the TPA must maintain while the contract is in effect
- Procedures for the final settlement of pending claims if the claim administration contract is terminated
- TPA's operating expenses if part of the compensation, types of costs considered expenses, and the calculations for those costs

4-3. Claim experience reports should include the following information:
- Results of the organization's loss investigations
- Organization's claim payments and receipts
- Information on pending and closed claims during the month

4-4. Warning signs of difficulty that might arise from a claim audit include the following:
- Failure of an organization's claim representative to respond promptly to questions or requests from the organization's risk management professional
- Inability of the claim representative to provide clear and reasonable answers to questions about specific claims
- Unexplained fluctuations in reserves
- Sudden increases in the number of litigated claims
- Steady increases in the number or value of pending claims
- Substantial increases in the number of justified complaints related to claims from any responsible source

4-5. Jessie should hire a qualified independent claim consultant to perform the audit because to perform the audit in-house would be a conflict of interest. Proposals from claim consultants should outline the audit's scope, plan of action, cost, time for completion, the identities of several clients for whom similar audits have recently been preformed, and the identities and qualifications of the individual auditors to be assigned to the audit. The proposal should also list materials required from, or tasks to be completed by, Jessie's department or other departments for the audit to proceed.

Educational Objective 5

5-1. Four ways an organization can reduce the costs of restoring its first-party and third-party claims are as follows:
- (1) Litigation management
- (2) Advance payments
- (3) Subrogation
- (4) Cost containment of medical claims

5-2. An organization should consider the following regarding litigation management:
- Legal counsel—risk management professionals might develop attorney guidelines, pre-screen attorneys, and select possible attorneys familiar with the types of lawsuits the organization might encounter.
- Legal bill audits—risk management professionals might review the legal bills to detect questionable billing practices.

- Alternative fee arrangements—risk management professionals might negotiate fees, such as fixed rates, flat rates, bonus fees, blended fees, or defense contingency fees.
- Defense plans and budgets—risk management professionals might outline the expectations in terms of what is to be accomplished and for what price.
- Status reports—risk management professionals might require status reports for initial and ongoing case evaluation.

5-3. The principles of subrogation are as follows:
- The party seeking subrogation has paid the debt.
- The party seeking subrogation has a legal obligation to pay the debt.
- The party seeking subrogation is only secondarily liable for the debt.
- A third party is primarily liable for the debt.
- No injustice is done by allowing the subrogation to be exercised by the party claiming the right.

5-4. The purposes of subrogation are as follows:
- To prevent the unjust enrichment of a third-party wrongdoer
- To prevent the windfall of a double recovery by the indemnitee
- To ensure equitable insurance price structures that properly allocate losses to those responsible

5-5. Two methods an organization might use to contain costs of medical claims are as follows:
  (1) Fee audits—by analyzing bills from healthcare providers, an organization can detect services not provided, those not properly provided, and those duplicative of other services. Fee audits can also identify improper charges.
  (2) Utilization review—by evaluating the appropriateness of treatment, an organization can identify unnecessary treatment and encourage alternative treatment.

5-6. One fact issue Janice should consider is whether the harm to the claimant is serious. In this case, the broken hip would certainly qualify as serious. Another fact issue to consider is whether some immediate cash could reduce the long-term consequences of the harm. This is a matter of personal judgment, but as this claimant is without medical insurance and without other clear means of financial support, she may not receive the necessary medical care to recover from this injury without financial assistance. Another fact issue to consider is whether legal liability is clear on the insured's part. The worn carpet did not happen suddenly and the insured knew many of its patrons would be trying to find their seat or would other wise be moving about in the theater when it was dark. It could reasonably be argued that repair of the carpet should have been a priority for the insured. Finally, does the claimant have a financial need and reasonable, cooperative attitude? As discussed previously, she does have a financial need. She also appears to have been cooperative by giving a statement to Janice regarding her version of the events and allowing it to be recorded.

Educational Objective 6

6-1. Loss reserves are amounts designated by claim representatives to pay claims for losses that have already occurred but are not yet settled.
  a. Underreserving gives management an unrealistically low estimate of true loss costs and could inflate management's estimate of the organization's operating efficiency. The organization might not have funds to pay for losses and might incur a loss of earnings on the reserved funds.

b. Overreserving gives management an unrealistically high estimates of claim values and could deflate management's estimate of the organization's operating efficiency. The organization might curtail activities or mistakenly think it cannot retain higher levels of loss.

6-2. The factors that make accurate claim reserving difficult are as follows:
- Type of claim
- Likely interval between initially reporting a claim and finally settling it

6-3. An organization might use the given methods of loss reserving in the following circumstances:

a. Roundtable technique—after evaluating a claim file, two or more claim staff develop a con- sensus reserve figure. An organization might use this method in serious or prolonged claims to review initial reserve amounts.

b. Average value method—amounts are based on data from past claims and adjusted to reflect current conditions. An organization might use this method when there are small variations in loss size for a particular type of claim and when claims are concluded quickly.

c. Formula method—amounts are calculated using mathematical formulas. The amounts might be based on an insurer's loss history with similar claims or as a percentage of limits of coverage.

d. Loss ratio method—an organization might use this method to establish aggregate reserves for all claims within a type of insurance when other methods of establishing loss reserves are inadequate.

6-4. Holly should explain to the CFO that open claims will ultimately have to be paid and that her best estimate of what each claimant will accept to release his or her claim is stated in each open claim's loss reserve amount. However, an additional amount needs to be added to the total for losses incurred but not reported as well as to the adjusting expense (referred to as allocated loss adjustment expense) that will be incurred to close each open claim. Holly should also give the CFO her best estimate of when these financial obligations will become due.

Direct Your Learning

Controlling Fleet Operations Loss Exposures

Educational Objectives

After learning the content of this assignment, you should be able to:

1. Describe the following aspects of fleets as systems:

    - Components and purpose

    - Environment

    - Life cycle

    - Systems relationships

2. Explain how to control the loss exposures associated with the following components of a motor vehicle fleet safety system:

    a. Vehicles

    b. Vehicle maintenance

    c. Operators

    d. Cargoes

    e. Routes

    f. Vehicle schedules

3. Identify the technological advances in motor vehicle fleet safety.

4. Define or describe each of the Key Words and Phrases for this assignment.

Study Materials

Required Reading:
▶ Risk Control
  • Chapter 9

Study Aids:
▶ SMART Online Practice Exams
▶ SMART Study Aids
  • Review Notes and Flash Cards— Assignment 9

Outline

▶ **Fleets as Systems**

  A. Components and Purpose

  B. Environment

  C. Life Cycle

  D. Systems Relationships

▶ **Risk Control of Fleet System Components**

  A. Vehicles

    1. Vehicle Selection

    2. Safety Equipment

    3. Vehicle Replacement

  B. Vehicle Maintenance

    1. Reducing Vehicle Losses

    2. Performing Maintenance Safety

  C. Operators

    1. Operator Selection

    2. Operator Training

    3. Operator Supervision

    4. Operator Licensing

    5. Operator Dismissal

  D. Cargoes

    1. Suitability to Vehicle

    2. Proper Loading

    3. Suitability of Routes

    4. Safeguards Against Inherent Vice

  E. Routes

  F. Vehicle Schedules

▶ **Technological Advances in Fleet Safety**

▶ **Summary**

▶ **Appendix A: Adverse Weather Guidelines**

▶ **Appendix B: Driver Pre-Qualification Form**

▶ **Appendix C: Driver's Application for Employment**

▶ **Appendix D: Record of Road Test**

▶ **Appendix E: Request for Information**

▶ **Appendix F: Request for Check of Driving Record**

▶ **Appendix G: Medical Examination Report**

▶ **Appendix H: Instructions to the Medical Examiner**

▶ **Appendix I: Checklist for Qualification of New Drivers**

▶ **Appendix J: Driver's Vehicle Inspection Report**

Plan to register with the Institutes well in advance of your exam. Please consult the registration booklet that accompanied this course guide for complete information regarding exam dates and fees.

For each assignment, you should define or describe each of the Key Words and Phrases and answer each of the Review and Application Questions.

Educational Objective 1

Describe the following aspects of fleets as systems:

- Components and purpose
- Environment
- Life cycle
- Systems relationships

Review Questions

1-1. Explain why an organization's risk management professionals should pay special attention to fleet loss exposures. (p. 9.3)

1-2. Identify the four common features of any system. (p. 9.4)

1-3. Describe desirable attributes of a motor vehicle fleet system. (p. 9.5)

1-4. Describe how the following environments might affect an organization's fleet safety: (pp. 9.5–9.6)

a. Physical environment

b. Legal environment

c. Economic environment

d. Competitive environment

1-5. Identify two implications for risk control and fleet safety management regarding system relationships in an organization's fleet system. (p. 9.8)

▶▶

Application Question

1-6. The management of Shirt Company, a shirt manufacturer, has decided their company will begin delivering its products to major retailers in the local area instead of contracting this service with a commercial delivery firm. Using the five-phase life cycle of a system, explain how Shirt Company's management and their risk management program can ensure appropriate delivery vehicles are selected and operate safely and efficiently.

Educational Objective 2

Explain how to control the loss exposures associated with the following components of a motor vehicle fleet safety system:

a. Vehicles

b. Vehicle maintenance

c. Operators

d. Cargoes

e. Routes

f. Vehicle schedules

Key Word or Phrase

Inherent vice (p. 9.25)

Review Questions

2-1. Identify the factors an organization should consider when selecting vehicles for its motor vehicle fleet. (pp. 9.9–9.10)

2-2. Identify the reasons why an organization might maintain a qualification file for each vehicle operator. (p. 9.20)

2-3. Describe the classifications of cargo loss exposures that a risk management professional should strive to control. (pp. 9.24–9.26)

2-4. Identify the factors that help an organization plan routes that will control vehicle motor fleet losses. (p. 9.26)

Application Question

2-5. Shirt Company will begin making local deliveries within the next six months. Propose an operator selection process that will set the groundwork for safe and efficient operation of the delivery fleet.

Educational Objective 3

Identify the technological advances in motor vehicle fleet safety.

Review Questions

3-1. Explain how technological advances in fleet safety offer
tools to control risks related to motor fleet loss exposures.
(pp. 9.27–9.28)

3-2. What could be the consequence of a risk management professional not acting on data captured by an onboard computer
that indicates a driver frequently acts in an unsafe manner?
(p. 9.28)

3-3. List the technological advances that assist an organization with
driver supervision. (p. 9.28)

Application Question

3-4.   Shirt Company has expanded its distribution area to areas throughout the east coast of the United States. Vehicle operators are on the road for longer shifts and operate with little direct supervision regarding safe driving practices. Explain how management, in their risk control efforts, might use technology to monitor and improve fleet safety.

Answers to Assignment 9 Questions

NOTE: These answers are provided to give students a basic understanding of acceptable types of responses. They often are not the only valid answers and are not intended to provide an exhaustive response to the questions.

Educational Objective 1

1-1. An organization's risk management professionals should pay special attention to fleet loss exposures for the following reasons:

- Potential for severe losses—motor vehicle accidents can cause frequent and potentially severe property, personnel, liability, and net income losses.

- Monitoring issues—directly monitoring the supervision and use of vehicles is difficult because they are used away from the owners' premises.

- Investment potential—motor vehicles are a major source of accidental losses, so an effective fleet safety program can be one of an organization's best investments.

1-2. The four common features of any system are as follows:

(1) Components and purpose

(2) Environment

(3) Life cycle

(4) Systems relationships

1-3. Desirable attributes of a motor vehicle fleet system are that the system be as follows:

- Reliable—completes trips as scheduled without harm to the freight or passengers

- Safe and well maintained—incurs few, if any, vehicle accidents losses that might increase transport time because of vehicle repair or maintenance

- Efficient—operates at an acceptable cost

- Environmentally neutral—does not pollute or harm the environment in ways that can impose common law or statutory liability

- Lawful—operates within the legal requirements of local, state, and federal laws

1-4. The given environments might affect an organization's fleet safety as follows:

a. Physical environment—highways, weather conditions, terrain, communities, and other forces encountered along a route can affect safe operation. Risk management professionals might provide safe operation guidelines in an effort to control losses.

b. Legal environment—laws regarding speeds, weights, hours of service, mandated equipment, and licensing tend to raise the level of fleet safety. Risk management professionals may need to spend time ensuring operation within the law.

c. Economic environment—during prosperity, fleet safety is likely to be financially supported. In recessionary periods, operators might speed, drive extra hours, or skip safety checks. In addition, labor union strikes and civil disorders might threaten safe delivery of cargoes.

d. Competitive environment—intense competition might lower fleet safety efforts and expenditures. These cost control measures could jeopardize the long-term safety of vehicles, operators, and their cargoes.

1-5. Two implications for risk control and fleet safety management regarding system relationships are as follows:

(1) When a smaller system fails, it becomes more likely that each of the larger systems of which the smaller system is part will also fail.

(2) Failure of the larger system degrades the environment in which its subsystems operate increasing the strain on those subsystems and the probability that they will fail.

1-6. Shirt Company might apply the five-phase life cycle in the following way:

- Conceptual phase—evaluate the types of delivery vehicles required, possible routes, and schedules

- Engineering phase—select reliable delivery vehicles, investigate hiring and training of operators, and finalize routes and delivery schedules

- Production phase—purchase the delivery fleet vehicles and hire operators

- Operational phase—conduct ongoing safety checks, vehicle maintenance, driver assessments, route evaluations, and schedule updates

- Disposal phase—review operators' and vehicles' safety performance and maintenance records and replace as needed

Educational Objective 2

2-1. Factors an organization should consider when selecting vehicles for its motor vehicle fleet include the following:

- Intended use of the vehicle
- Safety record of the vehicles
- Ease of maintenance
- Uniformity among vehicles

2-2. An organization might maintain a qualification file for each vehicle operator for the following reasons:

- To document the organization's care in selecting, training, and supervising motor vehicle fleet operators

- To be in compliance with applicable Motor Carrier Safety Regulations

- To identify the special training needs of each driver

- To evaluate each driver for pay raises or promotions

2-3. Classifications of cargo loss exposures that a risk management professional should strive to control include the following:

- Suitability to vehicle—some cargoes require special vehicles because of the cargo's characteristics, weight, corrosiveness, or toxicity.

- Proper loading—overloading or failure to properly secure cargo might result in cargo damage, vehicle damage, missed delivery schedules, or accidents.

- Suitability of routes—routes should present no unreasonable risk to the cargo and the cargo should present no unreasonable risk to properties or persons along the route.

- Safeguards against inherent vice—the vehicle must provide the appropriate environment for the cargo and that environment must be currently working.

2-4. Routes that help control vehicle motor fleet losses include those that are safe, cost-effective, reliable, reasonable in distance, and offer some flexibility if the main route is blocked or closed.

2-5. Shirt Company should first establish specific operator qualifications. In the recruitment process, company risk control managers might encourage the use of applications listing licenses, work history, and driving records, which can provide a method of pre-screening to eliminate unsuitable or high risk applicants. In the process of interviewing, the company's risk management professional might require administration of physical, written, and driving tests. Reference checks and verification of driving credentials should occur before the job offer is completed.

Educational Objective 3

3-1. Technological advances in fleet safety offer tools to control risks related to motor fleet loss exposures by helping an organization monitor and evaluate driver behaviors.

3-2. The consequence of not acting on the data could be that liability is imposed on the organization if the driver's unsafe behavior leads to the driver being involved in an accident.

3-3. Technological advances that assist with driver supervision include the following:
- Onboard computers
- Stability control systems
- Rear mounted video cameras
- Antilocking brake systems
- Onboard tire inflation systems
- Satellite communications

3-4. To establish safety monitoring methods, Shirt Company's management might install onboard computers that provide feedback regarding reckless vehicle operation and equipment malfunctions. If review of the data indicates consistent problems, additional training or vehicle maintenance can be implemented. When replacing vehicles in the fleet or performing scheduled maintenance, stability control systems, rear mounted cameras, antilocking brake systems, and global positioning systems might be installed to provide more detailed safety information to the driver that will improve the safe operation of the fleet.

Direct Your Learning

Controlling Environmental Loss Exposures

Educational Objectives

After learning the content of this assignment, you should be able to:

1. Describe the unique challenges of controlling environmental loss exposures.

2. Describe the key components of environmental risk control.

3. Describe the sources of, and types of harm leading to, liability for environmental loss exposures.

4. Describe the environmental loss exposures that might cause property, personnel, and net income losses.

5. Describe the following aspects of environmental risk control assessment:

   • Risk control assessment types

   • Risk control assessment factors

   • Risk control assessment uses

   • Risk control assessment process

6. Describe the following types of environmental loss situations:

   • Regulatory noncompliance

   • Discovery of contamination

   • Sudden or accidental event

7. Explain what environmental risk control measures are available, in what hierarchy they should be used, and what considerations are involved in their selection.

8. Describe four environmental risk control program considerations.

9. Define or describe each of the Key Words and Phrases for this assignment.

Study Materials

Required Reading:
▶ Risk Control
 • Chapter 10

Study Aids:
▶ SMART Online Practice Exams
▶ SMART Study Aids
 • Review Notes and Flash Cards— Assignment 10

Outline

▶ **Environmental Risk Control Challenges**
   A. Technical Expertise Required
   B. Differences Between Past and Present Losses
   C. Dynamic Nature of Losses
   D. Environmental Losses From Nonaccidental Events
   E. Time Between Event and Loss
   F. Regulatory Change
   G. Difficulty in Assessing Environmental Loss Exposures

▶ **Environmental Risk Control Key Components**
   A. Cross-Media Transfer
   B. Life Cycle Effect
   C. Nonpoint Sources
   D. Pollutants
      1. Metals and Metal Compounds
      2. Solvents
      3. PCBs
      4. Asbestos
      5. Dioxins
   E. Pervasiveness of Loss Exposures

▶ **Liability Loss Exposures**
   A. Sources of Legal Liability
      1. Torts
      2. Contracts
      3. Statutes
   B. Types of Harm Leading to Liability
      1. Spills and Leaks
      2. Legal Emissions, Discharges, and Waste Disposal
      3. Use of Substances
      4. Remediation Activity
      5. Indoor Air Quality
      6. Physical Changes

▶ **Other Loss Exposures**
   A. Property
   B. Personnel
   C. Net Income

▶ **Environmental Risk Control Assessment**
   A. Risk Control Assessment Types
   B. Risk Control Assessment Factors
      1. Characteristics and Behavior of Materials
      2. Pathways
      3. Populations at Risk
      4. Management Practices
      5. Mergers and Acquisitions
   C. Risk Control Assessment Uses
   D. Risk Control Assessment Process
      1. Create an Assessment Plan
      2. Assemble the Team
      3. Gather Information to Identify Loss Exposures
      4. Analyze Environmental Loss Exposures

▶ **Environmental Loss Situations**
   A. Regulatory Noncompliance
   B. Discovery of Contamination
      1. Proactive Response
      2. Prompt and Effective Communication
   C. Sudden or Accidental Event
      1. Twenty-Four-Hour Emergency Response Network
      2. Release Reporting

▶ **Environmental Risk Control**
   A. Source Reduction
   B. Source Treatment
      1. Recovery Processes
      2. Physical and Chemical Treatment Processes
      3. Thermal Processes
      4. Biological Processes
   C. Disposal
   D. Risk Control Measure Hierarchy
   E. Risk Control Measure Selection Considerations

▶ **Environmental Risk Control Programs**
- A. Compliance and Program Components
- B. Scope and Structure
- C. Coordination
  1. Production and Operations Management
  2. Management Information Systems (MIS)
  3. Marketing
  4. Accounting
  5. Legal
- D. Management Control
  1. Establish Performance Standards
  2. Compare Results to Standards
  3. Implement Corrective Actions

▶ **Summary**

The SMART Online Practice Exams product contains a final practice exam. You should take this exam only when you have completed your study of the entire course. Take this exam under simulated exam conditions. It will be your best indicator of how well-prepared you are.

For each assignment, you should define or describe each of the Key Words and Phrases and answer each of the Review and Application Questions.

Educational Objective 1
Describe the unique challenges of controlling environmental loss exposures.

Key Words and Phrases
Environment (p. 10.3)

Pollution (p. 10.3)

Review Questions
1-1.   Identify what the extent of pollution depends on. (p. 10.3)

1-2.   Identify the unique challenges of controlling environmental loss exposures. (p. 10.5)

1-3. Identify the personnel in the following areas that risk man-
      agement professionals might consult to help them identify
      environmental exposures: (p. 10.5)

    a. Internal and external resources

    b. Risk control team members

Application Question

1-4. Small Paint Company, located in a rural area of the United
      States, has been in the business of manufacturing paint for
      thirty years. Residential real estate development has rapidly
      expanded in the area. With the area's expansion, Large Paint
      Company is evaluating the possibility of purchasing Small
      Paint Company as a satellite location and expanding opera-
      tions at the plant. Discuss the environmental risk control
      challenges that Large Paint Company might face in taking over
      operations at Small Paint Company's plant.

Educational Objective 2
Describe the key components of environmental risk control.

Key Words and Phrases
Cross-media transfer (p. 10.8)

Life cycle effect (p. 10.9)

Review Questions

2-1. Identify the key components risk management professionals should understand to help them develop and implement environmental risk control measures. (p. 10.8)

2-2. Explain how the life cycle effect applies to a car battery. (p. 10.9)

2-3. Explain why a risk management professional should be aware of the environmental concerns that arise with the use of the following pollutants:

a. Metals and metal compounds (p. 10.10)

b. Solvents (p. 10.10)

c. Polychlorinated biphenyls, or PCBs (pp. 10.10–10.12)

d. Asbestos (p. 10.12)

e. Dioxins (pp. 10.12–10.13)

Application Question

2-4. In regard to Large Paint Company's evaluation of environmental loss exposures at Small Paint Company's plant, describe why risk management professionals should not only assess the hazardous substances currently used at the plant, but also consider possible loss exposures stemming from cross-media transfer. (p. 10.8)

Educational Objective 3

Describe the sources of, and types of harm leading to, liability for environmental loss exposures.

Key Word or Phrase

Remediation (p. 10.18)

Review Questions

3-1. Describe how environmental liability loss exposures might arise from the following sources:

a. Torts (pp. 10.14–10.15)

b. Contracts (p. 10.15)

c. Statutes (pp. 10.15–10.16)

▶▶

3-2. Identify types of harm that might lead to liability for environmental pollution. (p. 10.17)

3-3. Describe measures used by organizations to avoid site contamination. (p. 10.17)

Application Question

3-4. Although the population surrounding Small Paint Company's operation has historically been small, what types of environmental harm could lead to liability for Large Paint Company with the rapid residential expansion surrounding the plant?

Educational Objective 4

Describe the environmental loss exposures that might cause property, personnel, and net income losses.

Review Questions

4-1. Explain how an organization might incur property losses as a result of environmental pollution. (p. 10.20)

4-2. Explain how environmental pollution might result in personnel losses. (p. 10.20)

4-3. Explain how net income losses might arise as a result of environmental pollution. (pp. 10.20–10.21)

Application Question

4-4. Small Paint Company has received an administrative order from the Environmental Protection Agency (EPA) stating that the amount of atmospheric pollutants is above the permissible level. If Small Paint Company does not reduce this pollution to acceptable levels within six months, the EPA might direct that the facility be closed. Describe net income loss exposures that Small Paint Company faces because of this situation.

Educational Objective 5

Describe the following aspects of environmental risk control assessment:

- Risk control assessment types
- Risk control assessment factors
- Risk control assessment uses
- Risk control assessment process

Key Words and Phrases

Population at risk (p. 10.23)

Materials accounting (p. 10.25)

Compliance audit (p. 10.27)

Review Questions

5-1. Distinguish between the following types of risk control assessments and their common usage: (pp. 10.21–10.22)

  a. Quantitative

  b. Qualitative

5-2. What characteristics of a population at risk should a risk management professional consider when evaluating existing or potential areas of contamination? (p. 10.23)

5-3. Identify the ways in which an organization might use risk control assessments. (p. 10.24)

5-4. List the four steps in the risk control assessment process. (p. 10.24)

Application Question

5-5. Large Paint Company plans to expand Small Paint Company's operations to include production of a solvent that is highly toxic if inhaled or ingested. Describe how the appropriate risk assessment factors may be used to help Large Paint Company's risk management professionals assess this loss exposure.

Educational Objective 6

Describe the following types of environmental loss situations:

- Regulatory noncompliance
- Discovery of contamination
- Sudden or accidental event

Review Questions

6-1. Identify the general types of environmental control situations an organization is likely to encounter. (p. 10.29)

6-2. List factors that regulatory agencies might consider when enforcing violations of environmental regulations. (p. 10.29)

6-3.   Explain the benefits of an organization's open communication with the regulatory enforcement agency during the settlement process. (pp. 10.29–10.30)

6-4.   List the four goals of regulatory agencies regarding loss control. (p. 10.30)

6-5.   Describe the benefits of an organization's using a proactive response in efforts to reduce environmental exposures. (pp. 10.30–10.31)

6-6.   Describe the risk control actions an organization needs to take when a sudden or accidental event results in an environmental crisis incident. (p. 10.31)

Application Question

6-7. After Large Paint Company purchases Small Paint Company's plant and adjacent property, Large Paint Company discovers that the land on which the plant is situated is contaminated. What experts would Large Paint Company's risk management professional call in, and what would they do to develop a technical strategy and schedule of corrective action?

Educational Objective 7

Explain what environmental risk control measures are available, in what hierarchy they should be used, and what considerations are involved in their selection.

Key Words and Phrases

Source reduction (p. 10.33)

Source treatment (p. 10.33)

Solidification, stabilization, and encapsulation process (p. 10.35)

Review Questions

7-1. Briefly describe risk control measures that an organization might use to manage environmental loss exposures. (pp. 10.32–10.35)

7-2.   Identify basic risk control measures for source reduction.
       (p. 10.33)

7-3.   Describe how an organization might use the following source
       treatment methods to modify pollutants that have already been
       produced: (pp. 10.33–10.35)

       a. Recovery process

       b. Physical and chemical treatment processes

       c. Thermal processes

       d. Biological processes

▶▶

7-4. Identify the considerations that would influence the risk control measures that a risk management professional might select to manage environmental loss exposures. (p. 10.36)

Application Question

7-5. Large Paint Company's prior management bought 200 acres close to the company's largest production facility and spent a considerable amount of money to prepare the land so that it met Environmental Protection Agency (EPA) regulations for the disposal and storage of the toxic waste that Large Paint Company produces. How does this expenditure affect the hierarchy of the risk control measures that the current management of Large Paint Company should consider?

Educational Objective 8

Describe four environmental risk control program considerations.

Review Questions

8-1. Identify four considerations a risk management professional should address when developing an environmental risk control program. (p. 10.37)

8-2.   Identify the components an environmental risk control program should contain. (pp. 10.37–10.38)

8-3.   Identify functions provided by an environmental risk control program. (pp. 10.39–10.40)

8-4.   List the management control aims an effective environmental risk control program must have in place to ensure that the program is achieving its goals and responding to changing conditions. (p. 10.42)

Application Question

8-5.   Explain how the responsibilities and activities of the Small Paint Company's risk control program would differ from those of Large Paint Company's risk control program.

Answers to Assignment 10 Questions

NOTE: These answers are provided to give students a basic understanding of acceptable types of responses. They often are not the only valid answers and are not intended to provide an exhaustive response to the questions.

Educational Objective 1

1-1.   The extent of pollution depends on the type of substances introduced and the amount of substances introduced.

1-2.   The unique challenges of controlling environmental loss exposures are as follows:
   - Technical expertise required
   - Differences between past and present losses
   - Dynamic nature of losses
   - Environmental losses from nonaccidental events
   - Time between event and loss
   - Regulatory change
   - Difficulty in assessing environmental loss exposures

1-3.   Risk management professionals might consult the following persons to help them identify environmental exposures:
   a.   Internal and external resources:
      - Environmental compliance personnel—familiar with laws that apply to an organization's operations
      - Legal counsel—aware of regulatory loss exposures that must be addressed
      - Operational personnel—familiar with toxic and hazardous materials that the organization uses
      - Environmental consultants—assist with loss exposure identification through independent audits
      - Environmental Protection Agency (EPA) employees—external source that might provide useful information
   b.   Risk control team members:
      - Toxologists—to understand the behavior of material
      - Biologists—to evaluate the effects of pollution on environmental relationships
      - Industrial hygienists—to evaluate the risks of pollution on human health

1-4.   Large Paint Company might face the following environmental risk control challenges taking over operations at Small Paint Company's plant:
   - Past loss exposures—risk management professionals would need to investigate the substances, processes, procedures, disposal, and regulations used over the last thirty years by Small Paint Company to evaluate risk control methods used to manage the loss exposures from past operations.

- Nature of possible losses—risk management professionals would need to consider emerging trends regarding hazardous materials and assess how the residential expansion could affect local tolerance of paint manufacturing processes at Small Paint Company.
- Time between event and loss—risk management professionals would need to investigate Small Paint Company's disposal process and evaluate the potential need for cleanup in the area surrounding the plant.
- Regulatory changes—changing environmental regulations may require significant investment in pollution control equipment.

Educational Objective 2

2-1. Risk management professionals should understand the following key components to help them develop and implement environmental risk control measures:
- Cross-media transfer
- Life cycle effect
- Nonpoint sources
- Pollutants
- Pervasiveness of loss exposures

2-2. A car battery, which contains heavy metals and acids, has environmental loss exposures associated with its manufacture. New environmental risks arise once the battery's useful life has expired and the battery must be discarded.

2-3. A risk management professional should be aware of environmental concerns caused by the given pollutants for the following reasons:
   a. Metals and metal compounds—metals can never be destroyed, only managed in ways to reduce risks to human health and the environment through source reduction, recovery, and treatment.
   b. Solvents—mobility and diverse number of applications make solvents the most pervasive class of chemicals used.
   c. Polychlorinated biphenyls, or PCBs—although production and use is now banned in the U.S., PCBs can persist and accumulate in the environment.
   d. Asbestos—significant limitations exist on manufacture and usage, but in the past asbestos was commonly used in commercial applications. Asbestos may still be present in various products, such as heating and air supply systems and electrical appliances.
   e. Dioxins—difficult to eliminate once formed. Incineration is the only technology sufficient for destruction and removal.

2-4. Large Paint Company's risk management professionals should assess the hazardous substances used, including the treatment of hazardous substances and disposal methods currently used at the plant, because new threats and risks can emerge from previously used disposal or treatment methods. Large Paint Company needs to explore whether these methods have resulted in additional loss. For example, through cross-media transfer, pollutants (such as paint or solvents) that might have been contained and disposed of in metal drums buried in the ground, that could have corroded the storage containers over time and polluted the ground water or evaporated to pollute the air. The pollutants could have transferred to another media, rather than have been removed or contained.

Educational Objective 3

3-1. Environmental liability loss exposures might arise from the given sources as follows:

    a.   Torts—arise from any of the following:

- Negligence—failure to do what is reasonable under the circumstances to protect a third party from injury or damage
- Intentional torts—the most commonly alleged in environmental liability claims are nuisance and trespass
- Strict liability—arises from ultra hazardous operations or activities involving ultra hazardous materials

    b.   Contracts—might arise from hold-harmless agreements, merger and acquisition agreements, or as a result of a lease agreement

    c.   Statutes—can arise from local, state, or federal statutes, some of which impose strict liability

3-2. Types of harm that might lead to liability for environmental pollution include the following:

- Spills and leaks
- Legal emissions, discharges, and waste disposal
- Use of materials
- Remediation activity
- Indoor air quality
- Physical changes

3-3. An organization might use the following measures to avoid site contamination:

- Install spill collection systems
- Separate storm sewers from manufacturing sewers

3-4. With the rapid residential expansion surrounding the plant, Large Paint Company should be aware of potential physical harm to the area, which could lead to liability from the following causes:

- Spills and leaks—solvents used in the manufacture of paints could be unintentionally released through accidental discharge or machinery malfunction affecting areas not previously occupied, which could result in greater liability. In addition, the transport of material through areas that are now developed residential areas could lead to loss exposures if the transporting vehicle was involved in an accident.
- Discharges and waste disposal—Small Paint Company's disposal methods could have contaminated landfills which are now backyards and playgrounds. Large Paint Company could be liable for cleanup of these areas as well as for damages to harmed residents.

Educational Objective 4

4-1. An organization might incur property losses as a result of environmental pollution because legal and financial consequences of pollution cleanup can reduce the net value of a property and make it difficult to sell. Spills and leaks may also result in inventory losses for an organization.

4-2. Personnel losses might arise as a result of environmental pollution because occupational exposure to hazardous materials can cause chemical burns or other on-the-job injuries. Also, many work-environment contaminants have a cumulative effect on the body, resulting in illness or disease.

4-3.   Net income losses might arise as a result of environmental pollution because an environmental contamination event is likely to result in some business interruption, revenue reduction, and possibly result in negative press. Significant expenses can also be incurred in environmental cleanup.

4-4.   Small Paint Company might face net income losses because closing the plant would result in business interruption and revenue reduction expenses. Negative press regarding the pollution levels could also occur, prompting Small Paint Company to initiate a public relations effort to restore community confidence in the plant's safety, thereby incurring additional expenses.

Educational Objective 5

5-1.   a.   Quantitative risk control assessments identify and analyze numerical relationships between an exposure to a hazard and the actual occurrence of adverse effects to human health or the environment. These assessments are highly technical and expensive to conduct and are commonly conducted to specify allowable concentrations and exposure levels.

       b.   Qualitative risk control assessments identify and analyze existing and potential environmental hazards, rather than establish scientific cause-and-effect relationships.

5-2.   Characteristics of a population at risk that a risk management professional should consider when evaluating existing or potential areas of contamination are as follows:

- Amount and extent of potential harm
- Number of populations affected
- Population concentration
- Vulnerability of each population to the exposure
- Value that an organization or society places on the at-risk population

5-3.   An organization might use risk control assessments in the following ways:

- To improve the overall quality of the environmental risk control program
- To identify environmental liabilities assumed when property is transferred
- To determine the nature and extent of contamination
- To identify the best risk control measures to prevent further contamination
- For underwriting insurance

5-4.   The four steps in the risk control assessment process are as follows:

(1) Create an assessment plan

(2) Assemble the team

(3) Gather information to identify loss exposures

(4) Evaluate environmental loss exposures

5-5.   Large Paint Company's risk management professionals would want technical experts to study the characteristics and behavior of this material in terms of the toxicity of potential wastes, releases, and discharges; the process inputs, such as raw materials and catalysts; and any byproducts produced. Pathways through which the solvent could travel if released, such as by ambient air, soils, surface water, and ground water should be studied as well. Because of the close proximity of residential development, the populations at risk should also be studied in terms of population concentration and other characteristics. Finally, management practices should be studied. For example, what support can be anticipated or is needed from management for environmental loss control of this solvent?

Educational Objective 6

6-1.   Organizations are likely to encounter the following general types of environmental control situations:

- Regulatory noncompliance
- Discovery of contamination
- Sudden or accidental events

6-2.   Regulatory agencies might consider the following factors when enforcing violations of environmental regulations:

- History of violations
- Current operating practice
- Management practice
- Willingness to supply information

6-3.   Open communication with the regulatory enforcement agency improves the relationship with the agency and improves the organization's negotiation position. Failure to communicate or attempts to conceal information may result in stiffer fines, punitive damages, negative publicity, and possibly prison sentences for executives.

6-4.   The four goals of regulatory agencies regarding loss control are as follows:

(1) To ensure long-term protection of human health and the environment

(2) To meet all federal, state, and local environmental and public health requirements

(3) To ensure cost effectiveness

(4) To use permanent solutions to the greatest extent possible

6-5.   Benefits of an organization's using a proactive response in efforts to reduce organizational environmental exposures are as follows:

- The scope of cleanup and post cleanup care may be shaped early in the remediation process.
- The organization may have the best talent and capabilities to assess the situation and determine appropriate responses.

6-6.   In an environmental crisis incident, an organization needs to quickly take ownership of the problem, commit to its correction, and take responsibility for all those affected by the incident.

6-7.   Large Paint Company's risk management professional would likely call in technical specialists and engineering professionals to bear much of the risk control responsibility in managing a contamination exposure and cleaning up a pollution site. In nearly every case, an organization needs outside consultants to assist in the risk investigation and remediation effort. A site review, or preliminary assessment, is conducted to obtain information about the nature and extent of the problem. This is followed by a remedial investigation to understand the degree of risk associated with the site and to develop a technical strategy for cleanup. The remedial investigation focuses on contaminants of concern, cleanup requirements, regulatory agency requirements, and legal issues to be resolved. The remedial investigation may uncover additional data-gathering needs.

Educational Objective 7

7-1.   Risk control measures that an organization might use to manage environmental loss exposures include the following:

- Source reduction—reduces pollutants that emanate from an already existing source
- Source treatment—modifies pollutants that have already been produced
- Disposal—reduces the mobility of pollutants so that the waste meets land disposal requirements

7-2.   Basic risk control measures for source reduction are as follows:

- To change or modify equipment to produce less pollution
- To substitute hazardous materials with safer ones or ones that produce less pollution
- To redesign processes to produce less pollution
- To redesign products to produce less pollution
- To change operations or human behavior to produce less pollution

7-3.   An organization might use the given source treatment methods to modify pollutants that have already been produced as follows:

a.   Recovery process—separate, remove, and concentrate reusable material from the waste

b.   Physical and chemical treatment processes—reduce the volume of wastes, permit more economical and effective treatment, make waste less hazardous, and destroy toxic components of the waste

c.   Thermal processes—dissolve wastes either through combustion or pyrolysis (chemical decomposition caused by heating in the absence of oxygen)

d.   Biological processes—degrade chemicals through biological processes using formaldehyde, acetone, and isopropyl alcohol

7-4.   The considerations that would influence the risk control measures that a risk management professional might select to manage environmental loss exposures are as follows:

- The technical feasibility of the risk control measure
- The economic feasibility of the risk control measure
- The feasibility of the measure regarding environmental regulatory demands

7-5.   Normally, disposal would be the last option recommended in the hierarchy of risk control measures; that is, after all forms of source reduction and source treatment have been exhausted. However, as the cost of the disposal site has already been incurred, current management may view disposal as the most economical and still environmentally feasible method to use, despite the additional pollutants that would be produced.

Educational Objective 8

8-1.   When developing an environmental risk control program, a risk management professional should address the following four considerations:

(1) Compliance and program components

(2) Scope and structure

(3) Coordination

(4) Management control

8-2. An environmental risk control program should contain the following components:
- An organizational environmental policy
- A funding component
- A reporting system component

8-3. Functions provided by an environmental risk control program include the following:
- Ensuring that the organization complies with all applicable federal, state, and local requirements
- Developing and implementing policies, procedures, and standards pertaining to facility operations and ensuring that the organization meets all regulatory requirements
- Gathering, interpreting, and disseminating information about future regulatory requirements; improving the organization's ability to assess potential effects; planning for future developments; and avoiding crisis responses to situations
- Providing internal technical consulting services to managers, engineers, and technical personnel, enabling them to select and implement appropriate risk control technologies that meet environmental regulation requirements
- Increasing employees' awareness and understanding of an organization's environmental protection goals
- Educating employees and executives about environmental protection
- Improving communication with local communities, regulatory agencies, industry environmental councils, and other organizations
- Assisting, when possible, in developing regulatory policy and influencing the content of proposed environmental legislation

8-4. The management control aims that an effective environmental risk control program must have in place are as follows:
- Establish performance standards
- Compare result to standards
- Implement corrective actions

8-5. The risk control structure at Small Paint Company may have consisted of a few individuals who monitored compliance issues regarding environmental pollution. These individuals likely have other responsibilities in addition to keeping the facility in compliance.

Because the plant is a satellite location for Large Paint Company, they likely have a risk control group at its corporate headquarters that would oversee the environmental affairs at each of their locations. The risk control group would be devoted exclusively to environmental affairs and concerns at each facility. The members of the group would therefore likely not have other responsibilities that would detract from their primary focus on environmental issues. This group could seek economies of scale by identifying related areas of risk control and merging them together.

Direct Your Learning

Controlling Net Income Loss Exposures

Educational Objectives

After learning the content of this assignment, you should be able to:

1. Describe the variables affecting net income loss severity.

2. Describe the analyses used to assess property-related net income loss exposures.

3. Describe the risk control techniques and measures used for property-related net income loss exposures.

4. Describe the net income losses that can arise from liability losses and the risk control measures for liability-related net income loss exposures.

5. Describe the net income losses that can arise from personnel losses and the risk control measures for personnel-related net income loss exposures.

6. Given a case, identify net income loss exposures and select risk control measures to address each loss exposure.

7. Define or describe each of the Key Words and Phrases for this assignment.

Study Materials

Required Reading:
▶ Risk Control
  • Chapter 11

Study Aids:
▶ SMART Online Practice Exams
▶ SMART Study Aids
  • Review Notes and Flash Cards—Assignment 11

Outline

▶ **Variables Affecting Loss Severity**

   A. Length of Impairment

   B. Activity Level at the Time of Impairment

   C. Degree of Impairment

   D. Extra Expenses

   E. Length of Time to Resume Pre-Loss Revenues

▶ **Property-Related Net Income Loss Exposures**

   A. Assessing Property-Related Net Income Loss Exposures

      1. General Systems Analysis

      2. Subdivision Analysis

   B. Risk Control Techniques and Measures

      1. Prevent Property Loss

      2. Protect Key Equipment, Facilities, and Processes

      3. Devise Contingency Plans

      4. Replace Utilities

      5. Maintain Business Relationships

      6. Protect and Salvage Property

      7. Use Overtime

      8. Manage Extra and Continuing Expenses

      9. Plan for Post-Loss Communication

      10. Separate Key Aspects of Operations

      11. Control Contingent Net Income Losses

      12. Use Spare Parts and Equipment

      13. Use Outside Manufacturers and Suppliers

      14. Protect and Restore Vital Records

▶ **Liability-Related Net Income Loss Exposures**

   A. Products Liability-Related Net Income Loss Exposures

   B. Risk Control for Products Liability-Related Net Income Loss Exposures

      1. Prevent Products Liability Losses

      2. Devise Contingency Plans

      3. Recall Products

      4. Notify Customers

      5. Implement a Public Relations Campaign

   C. Work-Related Net Income Loss Exposures

   D. Risk Control for Work-Related Net Income Loss Exposures

      1. Implement Safety and Industrial Hygiene Programs

      2. Devise Contingency Plans

      3. Provide Prompt Medical Assistance

      4. Communicate Throughout the Organization

      5. Conduct Accident Investigation

      6. Provide Competent Temporary Replacements

▶ **Personnel-Related Net Income Loss Exposures**

   A. Key Employee Net Income Loss Exposures

   B. Risk Control for Personnel-Related Net Income Loss Exposures

      1. Implement Safety and Health Programs

      2. Devise Contingency Plans

      3. Cross-Train Employees

      4. Transfer Control of Business

▶ **Ardale Building Company—An Application of Risk Control to Net Income Loss Exposures**

▶ **Summary**

When you take the randomized full practice exams on the SMART Online Practice Exams product, you are using the same software you will use when you take the national exam. Take advantage of your time and learn the features of the software now.

For each assignment, you should define or describe each of the Key Words and Phrases and answer each of the Review and Application Questions.

Educational Objective 1
Describe the variables affecting net income loss severity.

Review Questions

1-1. Identify the variables that determine the extent of a net income loss. (p. 11.4)

1-2. Explain how the activity level at the time of impairment may affect loss severity. (p. 11.4)

1-3. Define a bottleneck and explain how a dual approach to risk control aides in controlling the degree of impairment a loss has on an organization's operations. (p. 11.5)

Application Question

1-4. For each of the following scenarios, select the most crucial variable affecting net income loss severity:

a. A bank branch located at a regional mall is damaged by fire.

b. A lobster boat is damaged when it collides with a pier, thereby laying the boat up during lobster season.

c. A commercial nursery that grows oak tree saplings from seed is damaged by flood.

Educational Objective 2

Describe the analyses used to assess property-related net income loss exposures.

Key Words and Phrases

Contingent net income loss (p. 11.7)

Extra expenses (p. 11.13)

Review Questions

2-1. Describe two types of systems analysis that a risk management professional can use to assess an organization's net income exposures resulting from property losses. (pp. 11.6–11.8)

2-2. Identify outside and inside entities that might affect an organization's operations. (p. 11.6)

2-3. Identify two types of flowcharts a risk management professional might use for general systems analysis and the usefulness of each. (p. 11.7)

Application Question

2-4. Food Grocery stores its perishable merchandise in a warehouse located two miles from the store. Explain how the development of a supply, marketing, and distribution flowchart might help Food Grocery to assess property loss exposures and to control property-related net income losses.

Educational Objective 3

Describe the risk control techniques and measures used for property-related net income loss exposures.

Review Questions

3-1.   Identify three risk control measures that an organization might implement after a loss to reduce the severity of a property-related net income loss. (p. 11.8)

3-2.   Describe the actions needed to develop an effective contingency plan. (pp. 11.10–11.11)

3-3.   Describe the measures an organization may use as part of the following risk control techniques to manage property-related net income loss exposures:

a. Loss prevention (pp. 11.8–11.9)

b. Loss reduction (pp. 11.10–11.15)

▶▶

c. Separation (pp. 11.15–11.16)

d. Duplication (pp. 11.16–11.17)

Application Question

3-4. The large swimming pool on the third floor of the ten-story Green Hotel collapsed without warning at 11:00 AM, causing several hundred thousand gallons of water to cascade through occupied meeting rooms on the hotel's second floor and the administrative offices and restaurant on the ground floor. In addition to the physical damage to the hotel, the rushing water injured hotel employees and guests and made the hotel's offices and restaurant unusable for an indeterminate amount of time.

Explain what the hotel's management should have done before the pool collapsed to reduce the severity of the hotel's losses from the following:

a. Physical damage to the hotel's buildings and contents

b. Interruption of its office and restaurant operations

Educational Objective 4

Describe the net income losses that can arise from liability losses and the risk control measures for liability-related net income loss exposures.

Review Questions

4-1.   List possible financial consequences of legal liability losses for an organization. (p. 11.17)

4-2.   What do the risk control techniques for liability-related net income loss exposures entail? (p. 11.18)

4-3.   Describe how an organization might incur a net income loss if one of its products injures someone or damages someone's property. (p. 11.18)

4-4.   Briefly describe how an organization might use the following risk control measures to manage products liability-related net income loss exposures: (pp. 11.19–11.21)

   a. Loss prevention

b. Loss reduction

4-5. Describe the circumstances under which an organization faces work-related net income loss exposures. (p. 11.21)

4-6. Briefly describe the risk control techniques and measures an organization might use to manage work-related net income loss exposures. (pp. 11.23–11.25)

Application Question

4-7. Danton Exterminating Company (Danton) is sued for applying chemicals in a more concentrated form than is recommended. Describe the possible financial consequences associated with this lawsuit.

Educational Objective 5

Describe the net income losses that can arise from personnel losses and the risk control measures for personnel-related net income loss exposures.

Key Word or Phrase

Cross-training (p. 11.28)

Review Questions

5-1.   Explain circumstances in which an organization could face a personnel-related net income loss exposure. (p. 11.25)

5-2.   Identify what affects the potential severity of a personnel-related net income loss for an organization. (p. 11.25)

5-3.   Briefly describe risk control techniques and measures an organization may use to manage personnel-related net income loss exposures. (pp. 11.26–11.28)

Application Question

5-4. Glass Art Company relies on two artesian glass blowers to create its products. Identify risk control measures Glass Art may consider to control its personnel-related net income losses.

Educational Objective 6

Given a case, identify net income loss exposures and select risk control measures to address each loss exposure.

Application Question

6-1. Abingdon Manufacturing Company has received an administrative order from the environmental protection agency of the state in which Abingdon's major plant, which burns coal for heat and power, is located. The administrative order includes a factual finding that the level of atmospheric pollutants from Abingdon's coal furnace is five times above the permissible level and indicates that, if Abingdon does not reduce this pollution to acceptable levels within six months, the agency might direct that the facility be closed.

a. Describe specifically (1) one liability exposure, (2) one net income loss exposure, and (3) one personnel loss exposure facing Abingdon because of this situation.

b. With respect to each of your three answers to a., describe two specific loss control measures Abingdon can institute to reduce the likelihood or severity of the losses from these exposures. Do not repeat any of your answers.

Answers to Assignment 11 Questions

NOTE: These answers are provided to give students a basic understanding of acceptable types of responses. They often are not the only valid answers and are not intended to provide an exhaustive response to the questions.

Educational Objective 1

1-1. The variables that determine the extent of a net income loss are as follows:

  • Length of impairment

  • Activity level at the time of impairment

  • Degree of impairment

  • Extra expenses

  • Length of time to resume pre-loss revenues

1-2. Many organizations have a peak season when their activity level is at its highest. A temporary shutdown at those peak periods could deprive the organization of a significant part of their annual income.

1-3. A bottleneck is any part of an operation that can shut down all or part of the business. Using a dual approach, a risk management professional can eliminate the source of a potential shutdown, or reduce its effects, and keep aspects of the operation unaffected by the loss running as efficiently as possible.

1-4. a. Because bank customers may change banks to another bank located in the mall in order to satisfy their need for convenience, the extra expense of opening a temporary bank would be the most crucial variable.

  b. Because lobster season is a set period, the activity level at the time of impairment would be the most crucial variable.

  c. Because it would take years for the nursery to regrow its stock, length of time to resume pre-loss revenues would be the most crucial variable.

Educational Objective 2

2-1. The following two types of systems analysis can be used by a risk management professional to assess an organization's net income exposures resulting from property losses:

  (1) General systems analysis—examines outside and inside entities whose impairment could affect one or more parts of the operation and cause a net income loss. The goals of general system analysis include estimating variables that affect loss severity, such as the length of impairment, the activity level at the time of impairment, the degree of impairment, additional expenses, and the time needed to resume pre-loss revenue levels.

  (2) Subdivision analysis—analyzes the organization's internal subdivisions, such as by building, by floor, by subdivisions of floors, by process, and by product. Advance subdivision analysis and planning can reduce a loss by having contingency plans in place before an accident occurs.

2-2. Outside entities that might affect an organization's operations include customers, suppliers, and utilities. Inside entities are the processes and operations themselves, including the raw materials and components, labor and management, and the equipment or other physical assets that are used.

2-3.   A risk management professional may use the following two types of flowcharts as part of a general systems analysis:

(1) Process flowcharts—show the physical layout of a facility and are useful for analyzing the facility's operations as well as the separations and concentrations of value within the facility. They can pinpoint aspects of operations that can potentially shut down operations, either partially or completely, and are useful for emergency response planning.

(2) Supply, marketing, and distribution flowcharts—display the relationships between the organization and outside entities such as suppliers, customers, and utilities. They can enable a risk management professional to estimate the effect of a contingent net income loss caused by a problem with the outside entity.

2-4.   Food Grocery's development of a supply, marketing, and distribution flowchart would display the relationship between the store, their supply of goods stored at the warehouse, transportation of the perishable goods to the store, and utilities providing services to the warehouse. From this, a risk management professional would be able to determine events that could potentially result in a net income loss and to calculate the effect of such losses on the organization's net income.

Educational Objective 3

3-1.   Three risk control measures an organization might implement after a loss to reduce the severity of a property-related net income loss are as follows:

(1) Protecting and salvaging property

(2) Using overtime

(3) Managing extra expenses

3-2.   The development of an effective contingency plan requires the following actions:

- Specifically assigning responsibilities and actions required to handle each contingency
- Providing written plans for reference and training purposes
- Regularly updating the plans
- Considering maintenance of manual capacity for automated operations

3-3.   The specified risk control techniques and measures may be used by an organization to manage property-related net income loss exposures as follows:

a.   Loss prevention—pre-loss measures to reduce loss frequency might include systems and procedures installed to prevent fires and explosions, proper building design, construction, and maintenance, and pumping and drainage systems for flooding. Measures to protect key equipment, facilities, and processes include plans to continue some level of operations until normal operations are restored.

b.   Loss reduction—pre-loss measures to reduce loss severity might include written contingency plans that specify procedures for predictable and unpredictable emergency situations, replacing utilities, maintaining business relationships, protecting and salvaging property, using overtime, managing extra and continuing expenses, and planning for post-loss communication.

c.   Separation—might include measures such as separation of key aspects of operations and controlling contingent net income losses.

d.   Duplication—might include measures such as using spare parts and equipment, using outside manufacturers and suppliers, and protecting and restoring vital records.

3-4. a. The hotel's management should have had a safety engineering inspection of the pool before the loss occurred to ensure that the floor structure under the pool could contain any damage and retain the water if the pool structure collapsed.

b. The hotel's management should have had backups of important records so that it could resume office operations immediately. The hotel should have had a contingency plan in case its restaurant was unusable. For example, many large hotels have multiple restaurants and separate catering operations.

Educational Objective 4

4-1. The possible financial consequences of legal liability losses for an organization include the following:

- Legal and investigatory expenses
- Money paid for settlements, verdicts, or fines
- Costs of complying with injunctions and orders for specific performance
- Loss of reputation or market share for the organization

4-2. The risk control techniques for liability-related net income loss exposures entail reducing the frequency, severity, and unpredictability of legal claims that generate net income losses and reducing the adverse effects that a claim may have on the organization's net income.

4-3. An organization might incur a net income loss if one of its products injures someone or damages someone's property because counteracting bad publicity, recalling the product, and starting a new marketing effort will reduce the organization's revenue and increase its expenses.

4-4. An organization might use the given risk control techniques to manage products liability-related net income loss exposures as follows:

a. Loss prevention—instituting pre-loss loss control measures before a problem arises to detect product defects in products under production. Loss prevention measures include reporting and responding to reports of unusual service or reliability problems, product misuse, or customer satisfaction.

b. Loss reduction—devising a contingency plan before a loss to coordinate implementation of loss reduction measures after a loss, such as recalling products, notifying customers, and implementing a public relations campaign.

4-5. An organization faces work-related net income loss exposures when employees are injured or become ill on the job. Expenses can result because of accident investigation, temporary replacement for the employee while the employee is unable to work, and reduced efficiency resulting from training a replacement employee.

4-6. An organization might use the following risk control techniques and measures to manage work-related net income loss exposures:

a. Loss prevention—pre-injury measures include the implementation of safety and industrial hygiene programs, which strive to prevent harmful exposures, prevent accidents, and protect workers' health.

b. Loss reduction—one pre-injury risk control measure is to develop a contingency plan, which defines how best to coordinate important post-injury controls. Post-injury controls include providing prompt medical assistance, communicating throughout the organization, conducting accident investigations, and providing competent temporary replacements.

4-7. Danton would be responsible for any damages awarded by the court if the lawsuit proved success-ful. Additionally, Danton would likely incur the following expenses:

- Legal and investigatory expenses—Danton would pay for legal fees, for testing where the incident(s) took place, and for experts who could testify on its behalf.

- Money paid for settlements, verdicts, or fines—in addition to damages, Danton may have violated state or local laws regarding the application of pesticides.

- Cost of complying with injunctions and orders for specific performance—Danton may be ordered to suspend operations until the proper concentration of chemicals issue is resolved.

- Loss of reputation or market share for the organization—Danton may lose significant amounts of current and future business because of this lawsuit.

Educational Objective 5

5-1. An organization could face a personnel-related net income loss exposure because of the death, dis-ability, resignation, retirement, or unemployment of key personnel who make major contributions to the organization's income.

5-2. The potential severity of a personnel-related net income loss exposure depends on the value of the work that the key employee performs; how much income the key employee generates; and the size, organization, and ownership of the business.

5-3. The nature and size of the business determines what risk control measures are applicable. An organization might use the following risk control techniques and measures to manage personnel-related net income loss exposures:

   a. Loss prevention—pre-loss risk control measures include safety and health programs that are designed to address injury and illness loss exposures at and away from work.

   b. Loss reduction—post-loss measures should be to return the affected employee to work, if pos-sible, or to replace the employee so that normal operations can be resumed. A contingency plan guides and coordinates all post-loss risk control efforts, such as cross-training employees and transferring control of business.

5-4. Glass Art could implement safety and health programs, which would reduce personnel-related net income loss exposures for all employees. Glass Art may consider hiring apprentices to learn the artistry of its existing employees.

Educational Objective 6

6-1. a. Abingdon is likely to face (1) liability for damage that the atmospheric pollution causes for downwind properties; (2) a loss of net income if this plant must close; and (3) personnel loss exposure if the Abingdon senior manager, who was most directly responsible for the environ-mental pollution, resigns or is fired.

   b. To control these potential losses, Abingdon can (1) make voluntary payments to owners and occupants of downwind land to mitigate their losses and to reduce their hostility toward Abingdon, (2) shift operations to another Abingdon facility so that any future closure of this plant will leave the company's net income substantially intact, and (3) take overall corporate responsibility for this incident so that the company's key executives feel less personal shame and less pressure to resign.

Direct Your Learning

Understanding System Safety

Educational Objectives

After learning the content of this assignment, you should be able to:

1. Describe system safety, its primary purpose, and the advantages to a risk management professional of applying system safety to risk management programs.

2. Describe the following features of a system:

   - Components

   - Purpose

   - Environment

   - Life cycle

3. Explain how to apply system safety analysis techniques to analyze potential accidents.

4. Explain how system safety analysis techniques and root cause analysis are used in accident investigation.

5. Define or describe each of the Key Words and Phrases for this assignment.

Study Materials

Required Reading:
▶ Risk Control
   • Chapter 12

Study Aids:
▶ SMART Online Practice Exams
▶ SMART Study Aids
   • Review Notes and Flash Cards—Assignment 12

Outline

▶ **Purpose and Advantages of System Safety**

▶ **System Features**
  A. Components
     1. Physical Elements
     2. Subsystems
     3. Energy Sources and Movement
  B. Purpose
  C. Environment
  D. Life Cycle

▶ **System Safety Analysis Techniques**
  A. Change Analysis
  B. Energy/Flow Analysis
  C. Prototype Analysis
  D. Job Safety Analysis
  E. Scenario Analysis
  F. Criticality Analysis
  G. Program Evaluation and Review Technique (PERT)
  H. Fault Tree Analysis (FTA)
  I. Failure Mode and Effect Analysis (FMEA)
  J. Technique of Human Error Rate Prediction (THERP)

▶ **Accident Investigation**
  A. System Safety Analysis Techniques for Accident Investigation
     1. Change Analysis
     2. Fault Tree Analysis
     3. Barrier Analysis
     4. Events and Causal Factors Charting
  B. Root Cause Analysis Techniques for Accident Investigation

▶ **Summary**

Use the SMART Online Practice Exams to test your understanding of the course material. You can review questions over a single assignment or multiple assignments, or you can take an exam over the entire course. The questions are scored, and you are shown your results. (You score essay exams yourself.)

For each assignment, you should define or describe each of the Key Words and Phrases and answer each of the Review and Application Questions.

Educational Objective 1

Describe system safety, its primary purpose, and the advantages to a risk management professional of applying system safety to risk management programs.

Review Questions

1-1.   Describe the primary purpose of system safety. (p. 12.4)

1-2.   Explain how a system safety approach to accident investigation can help a risk management professional control losses. (p. 12.4)

1-3.   List three advantages of applying system safety techniques to an organization's risk control program. (p. 12.5)

Application Question

1-4.   A passenger seated on a moving passenger train suffers a broken leg when the train comes to a sudden halt, throwing the passenger against the back of the seat in front of him. Assume that the train stopped because the engineer pulled the emergency stop cord as soon as he saw an automobile sitting on the tracks at a crossing approximately 100 yards ahead. Describe the nature and/or causes of this passenger's broken leg in terms of three levels of subsystems within successively larger systems.

Educational Objective 2

Describe the following features of a system:

- Components
- Purpose
- Environment
- Life cycle

Key Words and Phrases

Conceptual phase (p. 12.7)

Engineering phase (p. 12.7)

Production phase (p. 12.7)

Operational phase (p. 12.8)

Disposal phase (p. 12.8)

Review Questions

2-1.   List the four features common to all systems. (p. 12.5)

2-2.   Describe the components common to all systems.
       (pp. 12.5–12.6)

2-3.   Identify what a risk management professional needs to under-
       stand with regard to an organization's systems and subsystems.
       (p. 12.6)

2-4.   Explain what a risk management professional must do to pro-
       tect the integrity of an organization's systems. (p. 12.6)

2-5. Describe the five phases that occur in the life of any system. (pp. 12.7–12.8)

Application Question

2-6. A major automobile manufacturer is considering the development of a nuclear-powered automobile that could operate without refueling for up to five years on a uranium power pack placed in the car during its manufacture. With respect to safeguards against the harm that the nuclear energy in these cars might cause to persons and property, identify what the automobile manufacturer might consider during or while planning for each of the following phases in the life cycle of these automobiles:

a. Conceptual phase

b. Engineering phase

c. Operational phase

d. Disposal phase

Educational Objective 3

Explain how to apply system safety analysis techniques to analyze potential accidents.

Key Words and Phrases

Change analysis (p. 12.10)

Energy/flow analysis (p. 12.10)

Prototype analysis (p. 12.11)

Job safety analysis (JSA) (p. 12.12)

Scenario analysis (p. 12.12)

Criticality analysis (p. 12.15)

Program evaluation review technique (PERT) (p. 12.16)

Fault tree analysis (FTA) (p. 12.19)

Failure mode and effect analysis (FMEA) (p. 12.23)

Technique of human error rate prediction (THERP) (p. 12.23)

Review Questions

3-1. Describe the following techniques of system safety analysis: (pp. 12.10–12.11)

a. Change analysis

b. Energy/flow analysis

3-2. Describe the usefulness of prototype analysis to an organization's risk management program and the prototype criteria necessary to reveal potential hazards and defects reliably. (pp. 12.11–12.12)

3-3. Identify the four categories of failures that have been developed as a part of criticality analysis. (p. 12.15)

3-4. Identify the three steps involved in the program evaluation review technique (PERT) of system safety analysis. (pp. 12.16–12.17)

3-5. Identify the three steps in fault tree analysis (FTA). (p. 12.20)

Application Question

3-6. The following statements describe the circumstances surrounding the fall of a person on the wet marble floor in the lobby of the Franklin Building, a multitenant, high-rise office building, at 9:05 on a snowy morning:

(1)   The person fell because he was in a hurry, the floor was slippery, and his shoes had leather (that is, not slip-resistant) soles.

(2)   The floor was slippery because it was wet and the marble had not been treated with a nonskid wax.

(3)   The floor was wet because the Franklin Building maintenance employee responsible for keeping the floor dry was late to work and no one was assigned to fill in for him.

(4)   The floor had not been treated with nonskid wax because the wholesale supplier of this wax had been temporarily shut down by a major fire at its premises.

Describe four actions suggested by this fault tree that the management of the Franklin Building could take to prevent similar future falls.

Educational Objective 4

Explain how system safety analysis techniques and root cause analysis are used in accident investigation.

Key Words and Phrases

Root cause (p. 12.25)

Barrier analysis (p. 12.26)

Root cause analysis (RCA) (p. 12.27)

Review Questions

4-1. Describe the following in the context of an accident investigation: (p. 12.25)

a. Direct causes

b. Contributing causes

c. Root causes

4-2. Explain how the following system safety analysis techniques are used in an accident investigation: (pp. 12.26–12.27)

    a. Change analysis

    b. Fault tree analysis

    c. Barrier analysis

    d. Events and causal factors charting

4-3. Describe the procedure a risk management professional might follow when performing a root cause analysis to identify the most important cause of an accident. (p. 12.27)

Application Question

4-4. A boating accident occurred over the Fourth of July holiday when the bow of a boat struck the middle of another boat. Several passengers on the boat that was struck were seriously injured and one of the passengers drowned when he fell overboard. Drivers of both boats had been drinking alcohol. For the following three types of evidence, describe what should be obtained by an accident investigator:

a. Physical evidence

b. Human evidence

c. Documentary evidence

Answers to Assignment 12 Questions

NOTE: These answers are provided to give students a basic understanding of acceptable types of responses. They often are not the only valid answers and are not intended to provide an exhaustive response to the questions.

Educational Objective 1

1-1. The primary purpose of system safety is to address potential system failures before a loss and to provide a framework for investigating accidents that have already occurred.

1-2. Using a system-safety approach can help control losses because it allows a risk management professional to view accidents from the perspectives of many different systems. Each system suggests different ways in which the accident might occur and ways in which the frequency or severity of such accidents could be reduced.

1-3. Three advantages of applying system safety techniques to an organization's risk control program are as follows:

(1) Provides an orderly process for developing a range of risk control measures that improve the reliability of interrelated systems

(2) Enlists the cooperation of many people inside and outside the organization

(3) Reduces accident frequency and severity by defining and preventing events that lead to a particular type of accident

1-4. The passenger broke his leg because he was propelled forward with great force against a train seat. The passenger was contained with the subsystem of the train car. The train car itself is a subsystem of the train, which, with its locomotive engine, is pulling all the cars down the tracks. The train is a subsystem of the larger system of the railroad. In a more general way, this subsystem is contained within the entire transportation system of the United States. As an independently-operated vehicle, the automobile the train was braking for was also part of the transportation system.

Educational Objective 2

2-1. All systems have the following four features:

(1) Components

(2) Purpose

(3) Environment

(4) Life cycle

2-2. All systems have the following components:

- Physical elements—a system's ability to perform might be jeopardized by an impairment of a physical element.

- Subsystems—a system might be jeopardized when a subsystem fails.

- Energy sources and movement—a system is powered or moved by energy sources which can cause harm if not controlled.

2-3. A risk management professional must understand the following with regard to an organization's systems and subsystems:

- What all the organization's systems and subsystems are
- How these systems interact
- How the failure of any subsystem can endanger other subsystems and systems (including the entire organization)

2-4. A risk management professional must do the following to protect the integrity of an organization's systems by ensuring the controlled application of energy and the intended movement of a system's physical elements:

(1) Protect the ability of a system's parts to move as planned

(2) Ensure a reliable source of energy to power the organization's systems when needed

(3) Guard against this energy escaping and causing harm

2-5. The five phases that occur in the life of any system are as follows:

(1) Conceptual phase—when the basic purpose and preliminary design of the system are formulated

(2) Engineering phase—when the system's design is constructed and prototypes are tested

(3) Production phase (or development phase)—when the actual system is created

(4) Operational (deployment) phase—when the system is implemented

(5) Disposal (termination) phase—when the system reaches the end of its useful life and is disposed of

2-6. The automobile manufacturer might consider the following either during or while planning for the life cycle of the car in question:

a. Conceptual phase:

- How the automobiles can be manufactured and distributed without creating nuclear hazards
- How to "refuel" nuclear-powered automobiles
- Whether the public will consider nuclear-powered automobiles to be safe
- Whether nuclear-powered automobiles will endanger the environment

b. Engineering phase:

- How to safely manufacture nuclear-powered automobiles
- What portions of the manufacturing process should be automated in order to safeguard employees
- The ideal amount of nuclear fuel to carry aboard each automobile
- How nuclear-powered automobiles can be made sufficiently crash-resistant so that accidents do not release nuclear energy into the environment
- Whether the highway system needs to be renovated to accommodate nuclear-powered automobiles

c. Operational phase:

- How nuclear-powered automobiles should be marketed
- Where to locate nuclear refueling stations
- The feasibility of selling nuclear fuel through present gasoline distribution outlets

d.   Disposal phase:
   • How to safely dispose of nuclear-powered automobiles
   • Whether nuclear fuel cells for automobiles can have other uses

Educational Objective 3

3-1.   a.   Change analysis—projects the effects a given system change is likely to have on an existing system. It asks a series of "what if" questions and projects the consequences for each of the changes and for all feasible combinations of change.

   b.   Energy/flow analysis—analyzes the flows or transfers of energy within an existing or proposed system, checking for hazardous accumulations or escapes of energy. It is particularly useful to assess demands on a system, or set of subsystems, that is largely mechanical and whose failure is likely to result from some internal inadequacy rather than from human error.

3-2.   Prototype analysis is useful to an organization's risk management program because it provides an opportunity to discover and correct any defects in a product or process while it is still in its early engineering phase or before it is introduced in a new environment. To reliably reveal potential hazards and defects, the prototype must be sufficiently realistic, tested realistically in a representative environment, and subjected to detailed analysis before, during, and after the testing.

3-3.   The four categories of failures that have been developed as a part of criticality analysis are as follows:
   (1)   Category 1—Failure resulting in excessive unscheduled maintenance
   (2)   Category 2—Failure resulting in delay or loss of operational availability
   (3)   Category 3—Failure resulting in potential mission failure
   (4)   Category 4—Failure resulting in potential loss of life

3-4.   The three steps involved in the program evaluation review technique (PERT) of system safety analysis are as follows:
   (1)   Identify each event in a project
   (2)   Distinguish sequential events from nonsequential events
   (3)   Estimate the time required for each event

3-5.   The following are the three steps in a fault tree analysis:
   (1)   Identify the system failure as specifically as possible so all the events contributing to the failure can be fully described.
   (2)   Move down the fault tree from the system failure, and diagram the events that are necessary and sufficient to cause the events that immediately follow them.
   (3)   Determine whether the events leading to any other event on the fault tree are connected by an *and* gate or an *or* gate.

3-6.   Similar future falls could be prevented by taking the four following actions, as suggested by the fault tree:
   (1)   If the wholesale supplier had not had a major fire at its premises, it would have been able to ship the nonskid wax to the Franklin Building. The management of the Franklin Building should arrange for an alternate supplier of nonskid wax.
   (2)   If the employee had arrived on time, he might have known another way to keep the floor from being slippery. The building management, therefore, should have backup personnel for such circumstances.

▶▶

(3) If the floor had been treated with nonskid wax, the person might not have fallen. The management of the Franklin Building should have a supply of wax on hand at all times.

(4) Although management does not control the types of shoes that tenants wear or whether they run across the lobby, to have a marble floor just inside a high-traffic building entrance is not advisable because it can be slippery. The management of the Franklin Building should consider putting anti-skid material over the floor just inside the entrance of the building.

Educational Objective 4

4-1. a. Direct causes are the immediate event or condition that precipitated the accident.

 b. Contributing causes are events or conditions that do not individually cause the accident, but in combination with other causes, increase the likelihood of its occurrence.

 c. Root causes are the real cause of an accident or problem and not just a symptom.

4-2. a. Change analysis—examines what normally occurs, or what was expected to occur, and contrasts it to what actually occurred. A worksheet is typically used that specifies the what, when, where, who, and how of both the baseline situation and the accident situation. Differences are identified and assessed for importance in causing the accident.

 b. Fault tree analysis—determines paths of system successes and failures that caused the accident. A fault tree is constructed to reflect the situation and conditions leading up to the accident. This fault tree helps identify the interrelationships and details that must be considered when identifying the contributing causes of accidents.

 c. Barrier analysis—identifies physical, administrative, and procedural barriers or controls that should have prevented an accident. A worksheet is typically constructed that lists the barriers, how they performed, if or why they failed, and how that failure affected the accident.

 d. Events and causal factors charting—a graphical display, from left to right, of the sequence of events leading up to an accident. Data are arranged chronologically on a timeline, summarizing key information and depicting significant events.

4-3. When performing a root cause analysis to identify the most important cause of an accident, a risk manager might perform the following procedure:

 • Repeatedly ask "Why?" and trace the answers up the chain of command within the management structure to determine the failure points that allowed the contributing causes to exist and the accident to occur

 • Design a worksheet based on the chain of command within the organization and pose questions at all levels

4-4. a. Physical evidence should include pictures of the boats showing the point and angle of impact. The boats themselves should be preserved if possible. The empty containers of alcohol should also be collected. If the accident occurred at night, the investigator should determine whether the running lights were present and in working order.

 b. Human evidence should include eye witness testimony. Statements should be taken from each of the witnesses as soon as possible, whether they were in one of the boats, in another boat, on the shore, or in the water.

 c. Documentary evidence could include repair estimates for both boats, the medical records of each injured person, and wage loss information for any passenger who missed time from work as a result of their injuries.

▶▶

Direct Your Learning

Motivating and Monitoring Risk Control Activities

Educational Objectives

After learning the content of this assignment, you should be able to:

1. Describe the motivation process.

2. Describe the challenges of motivating employees to practice risk control.

3. Explain how management styles might differ applying the McGregor Theory X and Theory Y approaches.

4. Describe the following theories of motivation:

   a. Maslow's Hierarchy of Needs

   b. Herzberg's Two-Factor Theory

   c. Skinner's Operant Conditioning Theory

5. Explain how motivation theories can be applied to ensure employees practice risk control.

6. Explain how to monitor the effectiveness of risk control measures by controlling the performance of employees.

7. Explain how changes in the following can require modification to risk control measures:

   • Loss exposures

   • Legal requirements

   • Risk management priorities

   • Relative cost versus benefits of risk management techniques

8. Given a case, illustrate the types of changes that the results of risk monitoring might require.

9. Define or describe each of the Key Words and Phrases for this assignment.

Study Materials

Required Reading:
▶ Risk Control
  • Chapter 13

Study Aids:
▶ SMART Online Practice Exams
▶ SMART Study Aids
  • Review Notes and Flash Cards—Assignment 13

Outline

▶ **Motivating Risk Control**

   A. Challenges of Motivating Employees

      1. Differences Among Persons Being Motivated

      2. Differences Among Managers Seeking to Motivate Others

   B. Theories of Motivation

      1. Maslow's Hierarchy of Needs

      2. Herzberg's Two-Factor Theory—Motivators and Hygiene Factors

      3. Skinner's Operant Conditioning Theory

   C. Motivation Theory Application

▶ **Monitoring Risk Control**

   A. Controlling Performance

      1. Establishing Standards of Acceptable Performance

      2. Measuring Performance Against Standards

      3. Adjusting Standards for Below-Standard Performance

   B. Adapting to Change

      1. Changes in Loss Exposures

      2. Changes in Legal Requirements

      3. Changes in Organization's Resources

      4. Changes in Relative Costs and Benefits of Risk Management Techniques

▶ **Applying Risk Monitoring**

   A. Changes in Transportation Loss Exposures

   B. Changes in Risk Control Alternatives

   C. Changes in the Risk Control Measures Selected

   D. Changes in Risk Control Implementation

   E. Changes in Risk Control Monitoring

▶ **Summary**

For each assignment, you should define or describe each of the Key Words and Phrases and answer each of the Review and Application Questions.

Educational Objective 1
Describe the motivation process.

Review Questions

1-1.   Explain why motivating employees and monitoring risk control activities are important elements of a risk control program. (p. 13.3)

1-2.   Identify two reasons why a risk management professional might study motives and motivation. (p. 13.4)

1-3.   Explain how a risk management professional might change inappropriate behavior. (p. 13.4)

Application Question

1-4.   Despite the fact that all assembly line workers in an automobile manufacturer's plant are required to wear safety goggles, the employees consistently fail to wear their goggles. How would the study of motivation assist a risk management professional in correcting this situation?

Educational Objective 2

Describe the challenges of motivating employees to practice risk control.

Review Questions

2-1.   Identify the challenge for a manager in motivating the employees of an organization to practice risk control. (p. 13.5)

2-2.   Identify the challenge for a risk management professional in motivating employees to practice risk control. (p. 13.5)

2-3. Describe how the motives for fulfilling risk control responsibilities might vary depending on the following staff positions in an organization: (p. 13.5)

a. Front-line staff

b. Mid-level employees

c. Senior management

Application Question

2-4. Give an example of how a risk management professional could make use of the different motivators to encourage the following:

a. Front-line employees to report incidents

b. A plant's superintendent to attend monthly meetings of the plant's safety committee

Educational Objective 3

Explain how management styles might differ applying the McGregor Theory X and Theory Y approaches.

Review Questions

3-1. Explain why differences in the personalities of employees affects the ability of a manager to successfully motivate an employee's job performance. (p. 13.6)

3-2. Describe how a manager who subscribes to the McGregor Theory X approach motivates employees. (p. 13.6)

3-3. Describe how a manager who subscribes to the McGregor Theory Y approach motivates employees. (p. 13.6)

Application Question

3-4. Miguel, a shop foreman who is considered to be an effective leader, believes that the machine operators he supervises fit the assumptions of McGregor's Theory X. Miguel is attempting to motivate the machine operators to wear their goggles at all times while in the vicinity of any operating machine.

a. What actions would Miguel be likely to take to motivate machine operators to wear goggles?

b. How (if at all) would Miguel's actions described in your answer to a. change if, instead of Theory X, Miguel believed in Theory Y?

Educational Objective 4

Describe the following theories of motivation:

a. Maslow's Hierarchy of Needs

b. Herzberg's Two-Factor Theory

c. Skinner's Operant Conditioning Theory

Key Words and Phrases

Motivator (p. 13.11)

Hygiene factor (p. 13.11)

Review Questions

4-1. Identify the five major categories of needs presented in
      Maslow's Hierarchy of Needs theory. (p. 13.10)

4-2. Explain how employees might be motivated according to the
      following theories of motivation: (pp. 13.10–13.12)

      a. Maslow's Hierarchy of Needs

      b. Herzberg's Two-Factor Theory

      c. Skinner's Operant Conditioning Theory

4-3. Describe the four reinforcement strategies available to a man-
      ager according to Skinner's Operant Conditioning Theory.
      (p. 13.12)

Application Question

4-4. An assembly line worker at a chocolate factory is constantly sneezing at her workstation. An investigation determines that mouse droppings beneath the workstation are part of the problem. (The employee has been eating cookies on the job.) Explain how a supervisor might use Skinner's Operant Conditioning Theory to motivate the changes needed to address this situation.

Educational Objective 5

Explain how motivation theories can be applied to ensure employees practice risk control.

Review Questions

5-1. Explain how employees can be motivated to practice risk control. (p. 13.13)

5-2. Explain why different theories of motivation might affect the selection of controls to motivate risk control activities. (p. 13.13)

5-3. Identify what should affect the choice of the most effective consequences of unsafe behavior. (p. 13.14)

Application Question

5-4. For each of the following theories, describe one plan of action a manager could adopt to motivate machine operators to wear their goggles:

a. Maslow's Hierarchy of Needs

b. Herzberg's Two-Factor Theory

c. Skinner's Operant Conditioning Theory

Educational Objective 6

Explain how to monitor the effectiveness of risk control measures by controlling the performance of employees.

Key Words and Phrases

Results standard (p. 13.14)

Activity standard (p. 13.14)

Review Questions

6-1.   Identify two goals of monitoring risk control. (p. 13.14)

6-2.   Identify what controlling the performance of any activity entails. (p. 13.14)

6-3.   Explain why many risk control programs are evaluated using both results standards and activity standards. (p. 13.15)

6-4.   Identify external and internal sources from which risk control standards originate. (p. 13.15)

6-5.   Identify characteristics that are common to sound performance standards for any activity. (p. 13.17)

6-6.   Identify the conditions that must be met to measure and compare performance against standards. (p. 13.20)

Application Question

6-7.   The superintendent of a manufacturing plant is responsible for monitoring the efforts of various supervisors to minimize hand injuries to employees working at drill presses. In one department, in which Jones is the supervisor, the frequency of hand injuries has been low, despite the fact that Jones has not been holding the safety meetings, training sessions, incident recall interviews, or other measures that the superintendent has directed. In another department, in which Smith is the supervisor, the frequency of hand injuries has been very high, despite the fact that Smith has been diligent in applying all the measures ordered by the plant superintendent.

a. Identify the type of performance standard under which Jones's performance in controlling work injuries appears to be superior to Smith's and suggest two specific standards against which Jones's performance might be measured favorably.

b. Identify the type of performance standard under which Smith's performance in controlling work injuries appears to be superior to Jones's and suggest two specific standards against which Smith's performance might be measured favorably.

Educational Objective 7

Explain how changes in the following can require modification to risk control measures:

- Loss exposures
- Legal requirements
- Risk management priorities
- Relative cost versus benefits of risk management techniques

Review Questions

7-1. Identify types of changes that might stop a particular risk control measure being cost-effective. (p. 13.21)

7-2. Explain how a risk management professional can prepare and plan for possible changes in an organization's risk control resources.
(p. 13.22)

7-3. Explain the costs and benefits an organization should consider when selecting a specific risk management technique. (p. 13.23)

Application Question

7-4. For each of the following types of changes that may be necessary in a paper manufacturer's risk control program, give specific sets of circumstances that might call for the change:

a. Changes in loss exposures

b. Changes in legal requirements

c. Changes in the manufacturer's objectives

d. Changes in the manufacturer's resources available for risk management

e. Changes in the relative costs of alternative risk control measures

Educational Objective 8

Given a case, illustrate the types of changes that the results of risk monitoring might require.

Application Question

8-1. A restaurant owner decided to add a children's playground on the premises in the hope that it would attract more young families as customers. Focusing on the single new loss exposure of a child falling from some part of the equipment resulting in an injury, discuss the following:

a. Changes in risk control alternatives

b. Changes in risk control measures selected

c. Changes in risk control implementation

d. Changes in risk control monitoring

Answers to Assignment 13 Questions

NOTE: These answers are provided to give students a basic understanding of acceptable types of responses. They often are not the only valid answers and are not intended to provide an exhaustive response to the questions.

Educational Objective 1

1-1. Motivating employees is an important element of a risk control program because personal responsibility for risk control is essential. Monitoring is an important element because it helps an organization to determine whether risk control measures have achieved their desired results and to recognize and appreciate the value of risk control.

1-2. A risk management professional might study motives and motivation to explain past or present behavior and to influence future behavior.

1-3. To change inappropriate behavior, a risk management professional might create situations in which appropriate behavior is perceived to be more rewarding than inappropriate behavior.

1-4. Studying motivation would prompt the risk management professional to try to understand why the employees do not wear their goggles in order to determine what action to take to correct the situation. For example, the risk management professional may find that it is seen as a status symbol not to wear goggles—that is, the employees do not wear goggles in order to satisfy the need for status recognition. By introducing a bonus system that rewards adherence to safety standards, the risk management professional provides an incentive for the employees that could influence them to support risk control efforts by wearing their goggles.

Educational Objective 2

2-1. The challenge for a manager in motivating the employees of an organization to practice risk control is showing those employees how work can fulfill their personal needs in ways that also serve the organization.

2-2. The challenge for a risk management professional in motivating employees to practice risk control is to identify needs common to all employees and to create situations in which practicing risk control satisfies those needs.

2-3. Motives for fulfilling risk control responsibilities might vary depending on the following staff positions:

a. Front-line staff are likely to focus on risk control measures that protect them from personal injury, offer safety-related pay increases and bonuses, or provide awards and recognition from peers.

b. Mid-level staff probably respond best to motivators that are both personal and organizational and directly linked to risk control performance.

c. Senior management will probably focus on risk control measures that increase operating efficiency, improve the quality of the organization's products or services, enhance employees' well-being, or serve the general public.

2-4. a. A risk management professional could make use of the different motivators to encourage front-line employees to report incidents by stressing that avoiding these accidents will enable them to have more leisure time and ultimately increase the profits of the organization, resulting in higher pay.

b. A risk management professional could make use of the different motivators to encourage a plant's superintendent to attend monthly meetings of the plant's safety committee by emphasizing that the safety record of the plant will directly affect the profitability of the business and the supervisor's bonus.

Educational Objective 3

3-1. Differences in the personalities of employees affect the ability of a manager to successfully motivate an employee's job performance because motivation is an interpersonal process.

3-2. A manager who subscribes to the Theory X approach believes that employees are not trustworthy and are generally inferior to the manager. This type of manager gives very detailed instructions, supervises closely, and uses fear or threats of punishment to motivate.

3-3. A manager who subscribes to the Theory Y approach considers others equal and deserving of respect. This type of manager motivates employees to achieve their own goals and the goals of the organization by working voluntarily to fulfill responsibilities.

3-4. a. Miguel will require the machine operators to wear goggles near the machine, supervise them closely, and if cooperation is lacking, punish the employees who do not comply.

b. If Miguel believed in Theory Y, the actions described in a. would change substantially. Because Theory Y presupposes that people are not, by nature, passive or resistant to organizational needs, Miguel would emphasize the reasons for the employees to comply with the rules to wear the safety goggles. He will explain to the employees that they will be furthering their own goals of higher productivity, and ultimately higher pay, by wearing safety goggles.

Educational Objective 4

4-1. The five major categories of needs presented in Maslow's Hierarchy of Needs theory are as follows:
(1) Physiological
(2) Safety
(3) Belongingness
(4) Esteem
(5) Self-actualization

4-2. a. Under Maslow's Hierarchy of Needs, an employee can be motivated only if management can either appeal to an unmet need or negate a previously met need.

b. Under Herzberg's Two-Factor Theory, an employee can be motivated by achievement, recognition, responsibility, work, and personal growth.

c. Under Skinner's Operant Conditioning Theory, managers can directly or indirectly motivate employees to behave in certain ways by encouraging appropriate behavior or discouraging inappropriate behavior.

4-3. The four reinforcement strategies available to the manager according to Skinner's Operant Conditioning Theory are as follows:

(1) Positive reinforcement—the manager uses rewards, such as a bonus, time off, or formal recognition for satisfactory job performance.

(2) Negative reinforcement—the manager uses unpleasant methods, such as constant verbal reminders, to achieve the appropriate or desired behavior.

(3) Extinction—the manager discourages undesirable behavior by removing any previous incentives that may have been supporting such behavior.

(4) Punishment—the manager discourages inappropriate or undesirable behavior by using verbal or written warnings.

4-4. The supervisor may use any of the four reinforcers under Skinner's Operant Conditioning Theory to address this situation. A form of positive reinforcement that the supervisor could use is to implement a hygiene policy that rewards cleanliness at workstations with bonuses. Alternatively, the supervisor could use verbal reminders about workstation cleanliness as a form of negative reinforcement. Up to this point, eating at workstations has apparently been permitted. The supervisor could take away this permission as a form of extinction. Finally, the supervisor could punish failure to keep workstations clean.

Educational Objective 5

5-1. Employees can be motivated to practice risk control by controlling the consequences of their safe or unsafe behavior. Behavior that controls losses is rewarded and behavior contrary to effective risk control is punished or not positively reinforced with rewards.

5-2. The theory of motivation selected might affect the controls selected because each theory provides its own guidelines for influencing employee's safe or unsafe job behavior.

5-3. The choice of the most effective consequences of unsafe behavior should ideally be tailored to either the specific characteristics of the work environment or the type of behavior exhibited by the employee.

5-4. a. Maslow's Hierarchy of Needs—to motivate machine operators to wear safety goggles, the manager could emphasize the personal safety benefits of wearing the goggles and demonstrate that physiological benefits are met.

b. Herzberg's Two-Factor Theory—to motivate machine operators to wear safety goggles, the manager could emphasize the higher job satisfaction that the workers will experience, such as recognition and a sense of achievement.

c. Skinner's Operant Conditioning Theory—to motivate machine operators to wear safety goggles, the manager can influence the machine operators by rewarding appropriate behavior and punishing inappropriate behavior. The manager can dock the pay of anyone caught without safety goggles and can reward machine operators who have committed no safety violations.

Educational Objective 6

6-1. Two goals of monitoring risk control are as follows:

(1) To control performance (confirm that the chosen risk management techniques are implemented and are achieving their desired results)

(2) To adapt the chosen techniques to change

6-2. Controlling the performance of any activity entails the following:
- Establishing standards of acceptable performance
- Measuring actual performance against these standards
- Making adjustments either by correcting below-standard performance or by modifying an inappropriate (unattainable or insufficiently challenging) performance standard

6-3. Many risk control programs are evaluated using both results standards and activity standards because the casual connection between preventing accidents and reducing accident frequency rates is not always immediately apparent.

6-4. Risk control standards originate from the following sources:
- External sources—legal requirements and industry practices
- Internal sources—organizational policies and procedures and personal standards of managers and employees

6-5. Characteristics that are common to sound performance standards for any activity include the following:
- Consistent
- Objective
- Measurable
- Appropriate
- Stable
- Reliable
- Valid
- Flexible
- Cost-effective
- Exceptions-based
- Specific

6-6. The following conditions must be met to measure and compare performance against standards:
- Performance must be objectively measurable.
- Performance must be measured in ways and at times that are understood and accepted by those whose performance is being measured.
- Measurements must represent actual performance over the time period to which the measurements apply.
- Only significant deviations from performance should trigger managerial action.

6-7. a. Jones's performance probably will appear superior to Smith's under a results standard. Two specific standards against which Jones's performance might be measured favorably are (1) injury frequency or severity rate and (2) the cost of injuries per unit of output for his department.

   b. Smith's performance probably will appear superior to Jones's under an activity standard. Two specific standards against which Smith might be measured favorably are (1) in the number of safety meetings Smith has held and (2) the extent to which Smith's employees are able to describe (but not necessarily practice) approved work safety procedures.

Educational Objective 7

7-1. Types of changes that might stop a particular risk control measure being cost effective include changes in loss exposures, changes in legal requirements, changes in the organization's resources, and changes in the relative costs and benefits of risk management techniques.

7-2. A risk management professional can prepare and plan for possible changes in an organization's risk control resources by developing a list of priorities for existing proposed risk control measures and being prepared to drop or add measures depending on either decreases or increases in risk control resources.

7-3. When selecting a specific risk management technique, the organization should balance legality and ethical concerns and focus on measures that promise the highest internal rate of return or net present value of cash flows from the asset or activity to which each risk management technique is applied.

7-4. a. Changes in loss exposures—circumstances may include the organization moves into a new area, the number of shifts or hours of work of the organization is modified, or the means or routes of transportation change.

   b. Changes in legal requirements—circumstances may include a new statute, regulation, or court decision that demands a higher level of safety performance.

   c. Changes in the manufacturer's objectives—circumstances may include switching focus away from office paper into a new plant that manufacturers paper towels.

   d. Changes in the manufacturer's risk management resources—circumstances may include an acquisition, divestiture, or merger that causes an organization to develop a new set of risk management priorities.

   e. Changes in the costs of alternative measures—circumstances may include a change in the cost of insurance, new availability of risk control technology, or new safety regulations.

Educational Objective 8

8-1. a. The purpose of reviewing changes in risk control alternatives is to develop as extensive a list of specific risk control measures as possible for this new loss exposure so that no option is overlooked. Loss prevention and loss reduction appear to be appropriate techniques to consider. Installing a pad across the surface of the floor of the playground to cushion a fall would prevent or reduce injury. Installing netting on equipment that is more than a few feet above ground would prevent injury to a child who falls off the equipment. Installing a sign disclaiming responsibility may not prevent injuries but it may prevent a lawsuit for alleged negligence. Installing a surveillance camera to monitor inappropriate behavior could give the restaurant personnel an opportunity to prevent or reduce injuries.

   b. The projected costs and benefits of each of the potential risk control measures in a. need to be analyzed when selecting which measure to implement. The first three may be selected but the fourth measure involving the surveillance camera may be deemed too expensive and actually create an additional loss exposure of liability. The restaurant owner may be concerned that a parent would allege he or she relied on the restaurant personnel to use the camera to police the behavior of the children while on the playground.

c. The restaurant owner will have to select who will be responsible for buying the appropriate playground equipment. Vendors of the equipment will have to properly install the pad and netting. Specific restaurant personnel will need to be trained how to keep the area clean and should be charged with the responsibility of keeping the equipment in proper working condition and to report any required repairs and maintenance. Policies will have to be adopted to establish under what circumstances the playground would have to be closed.

d. To monitor the effectiveness of installing the floor padding and netting, these measures should be evaluated by activity standards and results standards. For both measures, an activity standard would be that they are installed. Results standards would indicate whether they actually prevented or reduced injuries when falls did occur in the playground.

Exam Information

About Institute Exams

Exam questions are based on the educational objectives stated in the course guide. The exam is designed to measure whether you have met those educational objectives. The exam does not test every educational objective. Instead, it tests over a balanced sample of educational objectives.

How to Pass Institute Exams

What can you do to make sure you pass an Institute exam? Students who successfully pass Institute exams do the following:

- Use the assigned study materials. Focus your study on the educational objectives presented at the beginning of each course guide assignment. Thoroughly read the textbook and any other assigned materials, and then complete the course guide exercises. Choose a study method that best suits your needs; for example, participate in a traditional class, online class, or informal study group; or study on your own. Use the Institutes' SMART Study Aids (if available) for practice and review. If this course has an associated SMART Online Practice Exams product, you will find an access code on the inside back cover of this course guide. This access code allows you to print (in PDF format) a full practice exam and to take additional online practice exams that will simulate an actual national exam.

- Become familiar with the types of test questions. The practice exam in this course guide or in the SMART Online Practice Exams product, will help you understand the different types of questions you will encounter on the exam.

- Maximize your test-taking time. Successful students use the sample exam in the course guide or in the SMART Online Practice Exams product to practice pacing themselves. Learning how to manage your time during the exam ensures that you will complete all of the test questions in the time allotted.

Types of Exam Questions

The Correct-Answer Type

In this type of question, the question stem is followed by four responses, one of which is absolutely correct. Select the *correct* answer.

Which one of the following persons evaluates requests for insurance and determines which applicants are accepted and which are rejected?
a.   The premium auditor
b.   The loss control representative
c.   The underwriter
d.   The risk manager

The Best-Answer Type

In this type of question, the question stem is followed by four responses, only one of which is best, given the statement made or facts provided in the stem. Select the *best* answer.

Several people within an insurer might be involved in determining whether an applicant for insurance is accepted. Which one of the following is primarily responsible for determining whether an applicant for insurance is accepted?
a.   The loss control representative
b.   The customer service representative
c.   The underwriter
d.   The premium auditor

The Incomplete-Statement or Sentence-Completion Type

In this type of question, the last part of the question stem consists of a portion of a statement rather than a direct question. Select the phrase that *correctly* or *best* completes the sentence.

Residual market plans designed for individuals who have been unable to obtain insurance on their property in the voluntary market are called
a.   VIN plans.
b.   Self-insured retention plans.
c.   Premium discount plans.
d.   FAIR plans.

"All of the Above" Type

In this type of question, only one of the first three answers could be correct, or all three might be correct, in which case the best answer would be "All of the above." Read all the answers and select the *best* answer.

When a large commercial insured's policy is up for renewal, which of the following is (are) likely to provide input to the renewal decision process?
a. The underwriter
b. The loss control representative
c. The producer
d. All of the above

"All of the following, EXCEPT:" Type

In this type of question, responses include three correct answers and one answer that is incorrect or is clearly the least correct. Select the *incorrect* or *least correct* answer.

All of the following adjust insurance claims, EXCEPT:
a. Insurer claim representatives
b. Premium auditors
c. Producers
d. Independent adjusters